50 FABULOUS
PAPER-PIECED STARS

~ CAROL DOAK ~

Martingale
& COMPANY

BOTHELL, WASHINGTON

DEDICATION

This one is for my mom, Mary Carlson, for teaching me to reach for the stars!

✳

ACKNOWLEDGMENTS

My heartfelt thank-you and appreciation are extended to:
Pam Ludwig for sharing the excitement of sewing paper-pieced star blocks.
My shining stars, Brian and Jeff, for being the wonderful young men that you are.
My husband, Alan, for being my best friend.
Ursula Reikes for saying, "Wow!" when I showed her the first few star blocks,
for all that she does so well as my technical editor, and for her friendship.
Everyone at Martingale & Company for their support and expertise.

CREDITS

President . . . . Nancy J. Martin
CEO/Publisher . . . . Daniel J. Martin
Associate Publisher . . . . Jane Hamada
Editorial Director . . . . Mary V. Green
Design and Production Manager . . . . Cheryl Stevenson
Technical Editor . . . . Ursula Reikes
Copy Editor . . . . Karen Koll
Cover and Text Designer . . . . Trina Stahl
Illustrator . . . . Laurel Strand
Photographer . . . . Brent Kane

50 Fabulous Paper-Pieced Stars © 2000 by Carol Doak

Martingale & Company
PO Box 118
Bothell, WA 98041-0118 USA
www.patchwork.com

That Patchwork Place is an imprint
of Martingale & Company.
Printed in China
04 03 02 01 00   6 5 4 3 2 1

Library of Congress Cataloging-in-Publication Data

Doak, Carol.
    50 fabulous paper-pieced stars / Carol Doak.
        p. cm.
    ISBN 1-56477-271-3
        1. Patchwork—Patterns. 2. Patchwork quilts.
    3. Stars in art. I. Title: Fifty fabulous paper-pieced stars.
II. Title.

    TT835 .D59 2000
    746.46'041—dc21   99-089521

MISSION STATEMENT

*We are dedicated to providing quality products
and service by working together to inspire creativity and
to enrich the lives we touch.*

CONTENTS

Preface · 4

Introduction · 5

Gathering Tools and Supplies · 6

Using Paper Foundations and Block-Front Drawings · 7

Selecting Fabrics · 8

Working with Grain Line and Directional Fabric · 8

Centering a Fabric Element · 9

Exploring Creative Fabric Options · 10

Paper-Piecing Techniques · 11

Measuring Fabric-Piece Size · 11

Cutting Fabric Pieces · 12

Step-by-Step Paper Piecing · 13

Sewing Assembly-Line Fashion · 16

Fixing Mistakes · 17

Completing the Block · 17

Joining Sections A and B · 17

Adding Fabric Across Sections A and B · 18

Joining the Sections · 19

Removing the Paper · 20

Mixing and Matching Sections · 20

Fifty Star Blocks · 24

Gallery of Stars · 25

Resources · 128

About the Author · 128

PREFACE

$\mathscr{I}$T WAS A simple beginning—divide the LeMoyne Star into eight sections so that beginning quilters could easily piece it. As I looked at the sections, however, it occurred to me that each of them could be broken down further into paper-pieced units. The quilt designer in me could not resist playing with the possibilities. I never dreamed that this idea would give birth to so many fabulous paper-pieced star designs.

 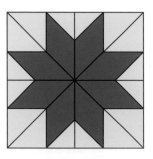

Traditional LeMoyne Star   LeMoyne Star in eight sections

Sewing the star blocks together was as much fun as designing them. It was exciting to see the stars come alive with color and texture. And they were so easy to make. I was thrilled that everyone would now be able to create perfect, intricate star designs with machine paper-piecing techniques.

As I was sewing the last few blocks for this book, my thoughts turned to how much fun it was going to be to teach paper-pieced-star classes nationally. I have been fortunate to travel to nearly every state in the United States to teach quiltmaking and paper-piecing techniques. I have received wonderful warmth and hospitality from quilters throughout the country. The memory of their kindness inspired me to dedicate a star block to the quilters in each state. The fabric choices for the star blocks were made to illustrate a variety of fabric choices and creative options and are not based on the state for which they are named. I dedicated the star designs alphabetically in the order they were made. I hope that the star blocks presented in this book will be a jumping-off place, and that quilters in each state will personalize the designs.

Dedicating one star to each state provides some wonderful design opportunities for creating special, memorable quilts. Below are just some of the quilts you can make using the blocks in this book.

* A family quilt using stars representing states where family members were born or raised

* A wedding quilt using stars representing the states of the bride and groom

* A group quilt where each member of the group makes the star for the state where she or he was born or raised

* A baby quilt using the birth state of the newborn child

* If friends are moving to another state, a star quilt representing their old and/or new state

* A quilt with stars representing all the states in which you have lived

I'm excited to share these star blocks and the easy techniques for making them. I can only imagine how many wonderful quilts will result from these as quilters embrace them and reach for the stars with their creativity.

INTRODUCTION

*E*ACH OF THE 12" star blocks in this book is created from eight paper-pieced sections. The designs may look intricate, but paper piecing makes it possible to sew these designs with absolute precision. After you've made just one star block, I think you'll see how great this technique really is.

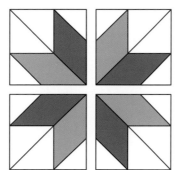

1. Start with
2 triangle sections.

2. Join the triangles
to make squares.

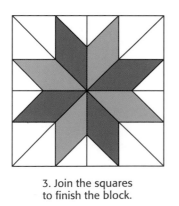

3. Join the squares
to finish the block.

In the back of this book, there is a free CD-ROM with a video presentation of paper-piecing tips and techniques. Now you can not only read about paper piecing these fabulous star blocks, you can also watch me show you how it's done on a computer running Windows 95, 98, NT, or better.

In "Gathering Tools and Supplies," you'll learn what items you need to make the blocks and to reproduce the foundations for paper piecing. In "Using Paper Foundations and Block-Front Drawings," you'll learn that you can use a copy machine to enlarge or reduce the paper foundations to make star blocks in a variety of sizes.

In "Selecting Fabrics," you will explore opportunities for choosing and using fabrics to create your star blocks. "Paper-Piecing Techniques" will show you how to paper piece. I will share the methods and tricks that I found helpful in making the star blocks.

In "Mixing and Matching Sections," you'll discover that the fifty star blocks presented in this book are only the beginning. You can mix and match the triangular sections to create many more fabulous star blocks. The design possibilities are endless. In "Fifty Star Blocks" you'll find a detailed cutting list for making one of each of the 12" star blocks, plus color photos to inspire you.

Whether you use one or more star blocks to make a quilt or a wall hanging, I hope you have as much fun paper piecing the stars as I did. Reach for the stars and allow the creative opportunities they offer to be the beginning of a whole new galaxy.

GATHERING TOOLS AND SUPPLIES

*H*AVING THE RIGHT tool to do the job can mean the difference between fun and frustration. The following items will make paper piecing the star blocks fun.

6" Add-a-Quarter™ ruler: This tool is invaluable for pre-trimming the fabric pieces.

Olfa rotary point cutter: Use this cutting tool to undo seams easily.

Open-toe presser foot: This foot provides good visibility so you can see the line as you are stitching. If you don't have one, don't worry; you can still paper piece. It's just a "nice to have" item.

Papers for Foundation Piecing: Use this lightweight paper when you copy the foundation piecing design (see "Resources" on page 128).

Postcard: Use a sturdy postcard to fold the paper back on the foundation before trimming the fabric pieces.

Rotary cutter and rotary mat: The large rotary cutter is the most effective with these star patterns, because you will often be cutting through four layers of fabric and paper.

Rotary rulers: The 6" x 12" and 6" x 6" rotary rulers are helpful for cutting the fabric and trimming the sections.

Sandpaper tabs: Place stick-on sandpaper tabs along the edge of the rotary rulers to keep the ruler from slipping on the paper when trimming. Place these tabs every 3" along the length of the ruler and ½" from the edge.

Scotch brand removable tape: This tape will be your new best friend if you need to repair your paper foundation.

Sewing thread: Use a standard 50-weight sewing thread. Match the thread color to the value of the fabrics. White, medium gray, and black can be used for most blocks. If one color is used in the center area of a star block, use that color thread. If both dark and light values are used equally, choose the darker thread.

Silk pins with small heads: Use these to hold the fabric pieces in place. They don't distort the paper and the small head doesn't get in your way when you are trimming the fabric pieces.

Size 90/14 sewing machine needles: The large needle will help to perforate the paper so it is easy to remove later.

Small light: This will be helpful when you want to center a fabric element in position #1.

Small stick-on notes: Label your stacks of cut fabric pieces with these. They will keep you organized and save you time.

Stapler and staple remover: Use a stapler to secure your foundations for trimming. The staple remover will save your fingernails when you want to take the staples out.

Thread clippers: This tool makes clipping the threads quick and easy.

Tweezers: Use tweezers to remove small pieces of paper caught in intersecting seams.

USING PAPER FOUNDATIONS AND BLOCK-FRONT DRAWINGS

*E*ACH STAR BLOCK requires four copies each of the section A and B triangles. One way to make paper foundations is to photocopy the designs on a copy machine. Be sure to make all the copies for your project with the same copy machine from the original designs. For a nominal fee, most copy shops will remove the binding of this book and three-hole-punch the pages or spiral bind it to make using it on a copy machine even easier.

You can also reduce or enlarge the designs on a copy machine to create the star blocks in a variety of sizes. The following photograph shows the Delaware Star in the original 12" size, as well as 4", 6", 8", and 15" to illustrate the creative opportunities enlarging and reducing the designs offers.

Use the following chart to determine reduction and enlargement percentages:

Finished Size	Finished Size	Enlargement or Reduction
Star Block	Triangle Section	% of Original
16"	8"	133%
15"	7½"	125%
14"	7"	117%
13"	6½"	108%
12"	6"	100% [Original Size]
11"	5½"	92%
10"	5"	83%
9"	4½"	75%
8"	4"	67%
7"	3½"	58%
6"	3"	50%
4"	2"	33%

Another way to make paper foundations is to use the *50 Fabulous Paper-Pieced Stars* Companion Software on your IBM or compatible computer to print the designs. See "Resources" on page 128.

The paper you use for foundation piecing should hold up while sewing and be easy to remove. If in doubt, test your paper by sewing through it with a size 90/14 needle and a stitch length of 18 to 20 stitches per inch. If it tears as you sew, it is too weak. If it doesn't tear easily when pulled after sewing, it is too strong. The paper does not need to be translucent. The light from your sewing machine is sufficient to see through the blank side of the paper to the lines on the other side. The Papers for Foundation Piecing from Martingale & Company work beautifully for these star blocks. See "Resources" on page 128.

After you make copies of sections A and B, cut the triangles ½" from the outside line. To do this

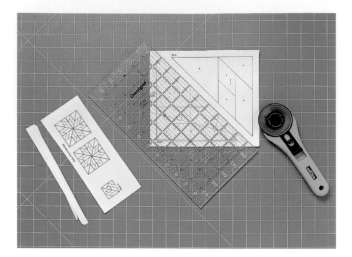

quickly and easily, staple the center of the papers together. Use your rotary ruler and cutter to trim the stapled foundations ½" from the outside line. Remove the staple.

The small block-front drawings at the bottom of the pattern pages show how the star blocks will appear when they are completed. Use the drawings to experiment with color and design choices or avenues. I like to use the term "avenue," because it suggests a direction for the decisions you make about color and value placement in the star block. One set of decisions can result in a very different looking star block from another set of decisions.

SELECTING FABRICS

𝒴OUR FABRIC CHOICES will bring your paper-pieced star blocks to life, but you are not limited to 100 percent cotton fabrics. One of the advantages to paper piecing is that you can use other fabrics, such as silk, satin, and lamé, in your blocks.

Working with Grain Line and Directional Fabric

BECAUSE YOU ARE paper piecing, you do not need to concern yourself with fabric grain for mechanical reasons. The paper supports the fabric no matter how it is placed on the foundation. Visually, however, the grain line and the print on the fabric do have an impact on the finished block. For this reason, the background triangles are cut as half-square triangles so that the grain line and the print will be consistent along the edges of the block. The

larger the fabric pieces, the more important it is to keep this consistency.

Start with a square of background fabric.

Cut it in half to make half-square triangles.

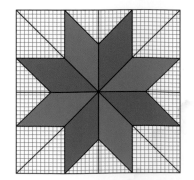

Position the triangles so that the grain line and printed pattern are consistent throughout the block.

Select solid and non-directional printed fabrics for the background of the diamonds. Using a directional fabric is distracting because the grain line and print will be going in different directions.

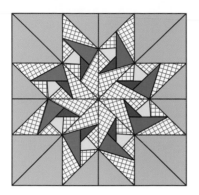

Directional fabric used in the background
of the star points is distracting.

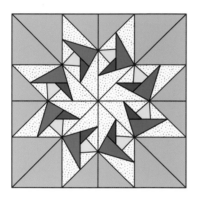

Non-directional fabric used in
the background of the star points

You can use a directional fabric, such as a stripe, for a design element inside the diamond because its use will be consistent in each section. Cut across the stripe rather than with the stripe to make any slight differences in fabric positioning less noticeable.

Centering a Fabric Element

CENTERING A FABRIC element in area #1 creates interest and adds detail. I used this technique in the Alaska, California, Montana, New York, and Tennessee star blocks.

1. Trace the size and shape of area #1 onto a piece of translucent tracing paper. Make a mark to indicate the direction in which you want to position the motif.

2. Cut out the traced shape with a ½" seam allowance all around.

3. Place the traced shape, marked side down, on the right side of the fabric and move it around the fabric to explore which images fit within the shape.

4. When you settle on a fabric element, trace the general shape of the element on the tracing paper. This will assist you in placing the tracing paper on the same fabric element for additional required pieces. Cut the areas out of the fabric following the outside edge of the paper as a guide.

5. Use a small light to help you center the fabric element in the same place in area #1 on each paper foundation. Pin it in place and begin paper piecing.

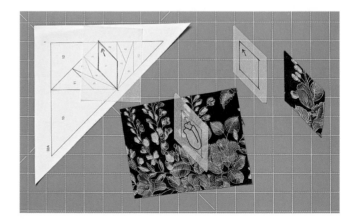

Exploring Creative Fabric Options

YOUR CHOICE OF fabrics can set a theme, create a graphic impact or add extra detail in your star block. Start by selecting the fabric for the background of the star. Frequently I look for a "main player" fabric that I love and then select the remainder of the fabrics based on the colors in the main player fabric. The photograph below shows a main player fabric in front of a group of potential fabrics that possess a variety of values, colors, and textures.

You can dramatically alter the look of a star by changing color and value placement. The star blocks that I made are examples of the decisions I made about color and value on a particular day. However, the next time I make the same block, I can choose to arrange colors and values in a different way. Use the block-front drawings to explore different design avenues. Let's use the New Jersey star to illustrate this point. What color and value placement avenue do you see?

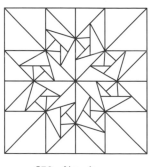

S30   New Jersey

The following illustration shows how I placed color and value when I made the sample block on page 86.

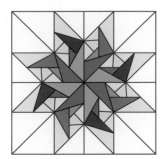

I used this design avenue for
the star block example that I made.

Look at the possibilities for this star block when you change the color and value placements.

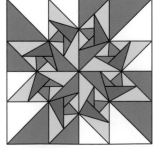

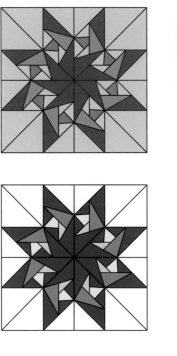

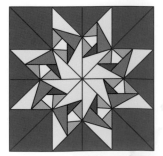

Amazing, isn't it!

You can emphasize the diamond portion of the star by having a high contrast between the diamond and the background fabric. To de-emphasize the diamonds, use the same fabric for part of the diamond and the background of the block.

Diamonds are evident.

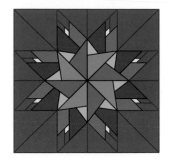
Diamonds are not evident.

Once you have a plan for color and value placement in the block, your next step is to select the fabrics. I know that many quilters agonize over choosing fabric combinations for their patchwork. However, this does not need to be a frustrating experience, and I've even developed a technique to help you make those color and value choices.

Because I am a visual person, I like to see how the fabrics will work together before I sew the block. To help me visualize this, I simply fold and position the fabrics in the intended areas of the triangle section. Let's look at how I auditioned fabrics for the following triangle. I start by placing a square of fabric on a table for the background. Next, I place the fabric for the diamond portion of the star across it and then position the design elements as they will be used. This gives me a perspective of how the fabrics will appear next to each other in the block. If I don't like what I see I can switch the position of the fabrics, or audition new fabrics until I find a combination that I like. If you find choosing fabrics an uneasy process, you might want to try this technique.

PAPER-PIECING TECHNIQUES

Measuring Fabric-Piece Size

THE GOOD NEWS is that there is a cutting list for making one of each 12" star block. The measurements are generous to allow room for easy placement and any shifting that might occur while you sew.

However, if you decide to enlarge or reduce the designs, you will want to know how to measure the fabric pieces. To measure the first piece, place a rotary ruler over the area marked #1 in the same manner you will place fabric #1. You can see how big the fabric piece needs to be, including a generous seam allowance. I allow at least ¾" total for seam allowances.

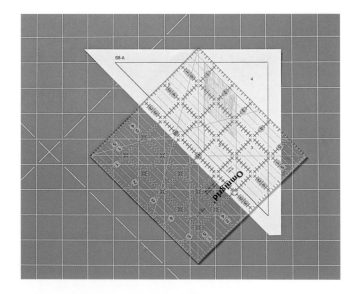

To measure subsequent fabric pieces, align the ¼" line on the rotary ruler with the seam you will sew and let the ruler fall over the area of the next piece. Look through the ruler to see how big the piece needs to be, including a generous seam allowance on all sides.

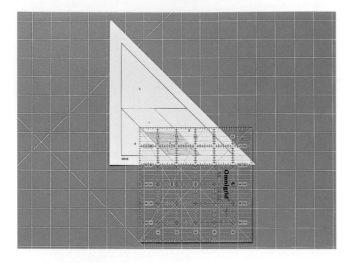

For half-square triangles, measure the short side of the triangle and add 1¼" to that measurement. Cut a square the size of the short side of the triangle plus 1¼" and cut it once diagonally. If you are using a one-way directional print, see facing page.

The short side measures 3½".
Add 1¼" for seam allowances.
Cut square 4¾" x 4¾" and
cut in half diagonally to make
two half-square triangles.

The short side measures 2½".
Add 1¼" for seam allowances.
Cut square 3¾" x 3¾" and
cut in half diagonally to make
two half-square triangles.

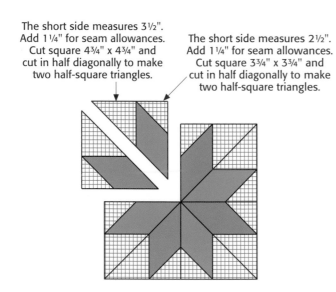

Cutting Fabric Pieces

ONCE YOUR FABRIC is selected, it is time to rotary cut your fabric pieces. Remember, each star block has a cutting list for the fabric pieces. If you'd prefer different colors from the ones listed, simply substitute your fabric choices for the ones in the chart.

To cut several pieces at one time, fold the fabric twice and cut a strip across the width. If you need only a few pieces, cut a shorter strip.

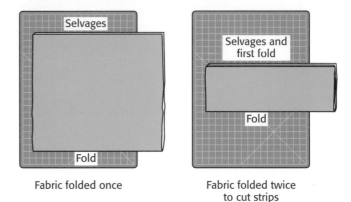

Fabric folded once

Fabric folded twice
to cut strips

As the pieces are cut, label them with stick-on notes to indicate the location number and section. Since the fabric is folded, the pieces will be right side up and wrong side up. Take the time to arrange them so that they are all right side up. This way, you won't need to check each one as you are paper piecing.

Many of the star blocks require half-square triangles for the background triangles. These are easily cut from 4¾" and 3¾" squares. Fold the fabric twice and cut a 4¾"-wide strip across the width. Turn the strip and remove the fold and selvage edges. Cut four squares, 4¾" x 4¾". Remember, since you're cutting four layers of fabric at a time, you will be cutting four squares at once. Cut the squares once diagonally to make eight triangles. Cut four squares, 3¾" x 3¾", from the remainder of the strip, and cut once diagonally to make another eight triangles.

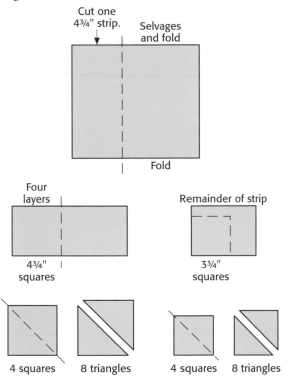

If you decide to use a one-way directional fabric for the background triangles, cut the squares from a strip of fabric as described above. With like sides (either right sides or wrong sides) together, cut the squares once diagonally. Paper piece the eight sections, but do not add the background triangles yet. Lay out the A and B sections to form the star. Then position the triangles so that the print is oriented correctly. Stitch the triangles in place.

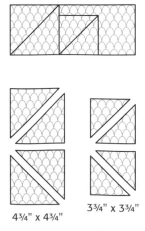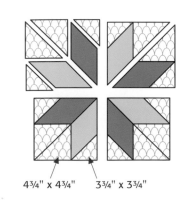

After the fabric pieces are cut and labeled, place them on a tray in numerical order. This allows you to move them easily from the cutting table to the sewing machine. If the same fabric pieces are used in both sections A and B, place them in numerical order. If different fabric pieces are used in sections A and B, place them in the appropriate group.

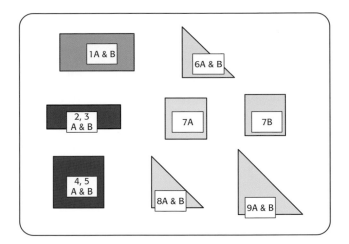

Step-by-Step Paper Piecing

WITH YOUR FOUNDATIONS copied and trimmed, your fabric selected, cut and labeled, you are now ready to begin paper piecing the sections for your star block. The numbered and lined side of the foundation is the reverse (or mirror image) of the finished block. This often confuses beginners to paper piecing because they look at the lined side and try to think in reverse. The key is to look through the blank side of the foundation to the lines on the other side. This way, what you see is what you get, and you do not need to think in reverse.

In the following photographs, translucent tracing paper is used as the foundation for the Delaware Star block, Section A, so you can see the lines through the blank side of the paper.

1. Use a size 90/14 sewing machine needle, an open-toe presser foot for good visibility, and a stitch length of 18 to 20 stitches per inch. The larger needle and the smaller stitch length will aid you in removing the paper easily.

2. Using the light on your sewing machine, look through the blank side of the paper to place fabric piece #1 right side up over the area marked #1. Make sure it covers area #1 and extends at least ¼" beyond all seam lines. Pin in place.

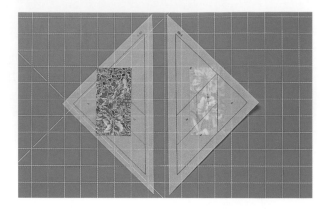

3. Place the postcard on the line between #1 and #2, and fold the paper back to expose the excess fabric beyond the seam line.

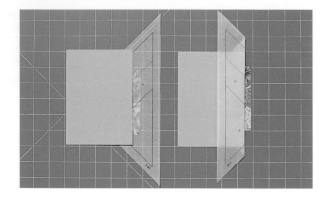

4. Place an Add-a-Quarter ruler on the fold and trim the excess fabric ¼" from the fold. The lip on this ruler prevents it from slipping as you trim. Or you can align the ¼" line on a rotary ruler with the fold to trim.

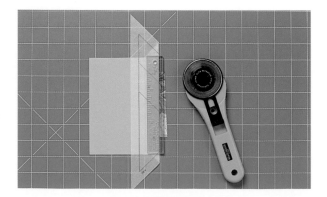

5. Looking through the blank side of the paper to the design on the other side, place fabric #2 RIGHT side up over area #2. This is an important step. The reason you want to look through the blank side of the paper to position the next piece of fabric is to see how the fabric will appear when it is sewn. Remember, what you see is what you get.

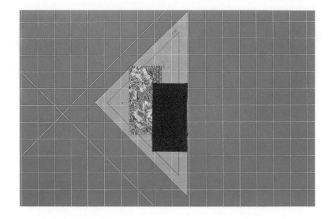

After piece #2 is properly positioned, flip it right sides together with the just-trimmed edge of piece #1. Looking through the blank side of the paper again, check that the end of piece #2 extends beyond the end of the seam line of piece #2 on the foundation.

If you are using cotton fabric, this piece should cling to piece #1, but if it makes you feel more comfortable you can pin piece #2 in place. If you use slippery fabrics, definitely pin this piece in place.

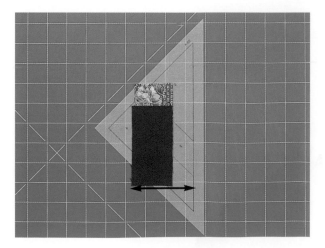

6. Place the foundation under the presser foot and sew on the seam line between #1 and #2, beginning about ¼" before the seam and extending the stitching about ¼" beyond the end of the seam line.

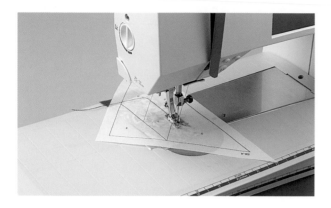

7. Remove the pin and open piece #2. If you are using cotton fabrics, press with a dry iron on a cotton setting. If you are using heat sensitive fabrics, use a pressing cloth or lower the temperature on the iron. Cover your ironing surface with a piece of scrap fabric to protect it from any ink that may transfer from photocopies.

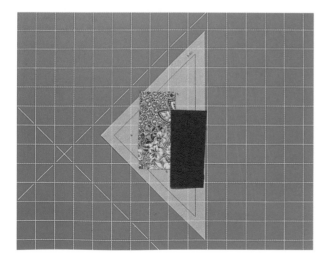

8. Place the postcard on the next line you will sew. This is where line #3 adjoins the previous pieces. Fold the paper back, exposing the excess fabric. If necessary, pull the stitches away from the paper foundation to fold the paper. Place the Add-a-Quarter ruler on the fold and trim ¼" from the fold.

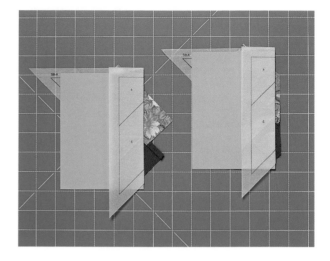

9. Place fabric #3 RIGHT side up over area #3 to check for proper placement. Place the fabric right sides together with the just-trimmed edges of pieces #1 and #2. See how the fabric extends to cover the center point of the section plus seam allowance? Sew and press open.

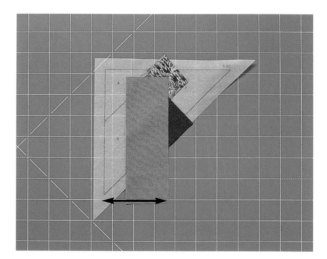

10. Continue with piece #4 by placing the postcard on the line between #1/#3 and #4. Fold the paper back and trim the excess fabrics ¼" from the fold. Place triangle #4 RIGHT side up over area #4 to check for placement, and then flip it right sides together along the just-trimmed edge. Align the corner of the fabric triangle with the corner of the triangle printed on the foundation. Sew and press open.

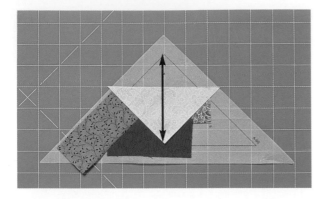

11. Place the postcard on the line between #1/#2 and #5. Fold the paper back and trim the excess fabrics ¼" from the fold. Place triangle #5 RIGHT side up over area #5 to check for placement, and then flip it right sides together along the just-trimmed edge. Center the triangle so the edge extends at least ¼" beyond the outside line. Sew and press open.

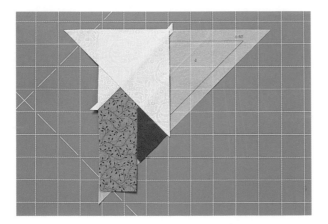

12. Trim the foundation ¼" from the outside line as follows:

A. Trim the long side of the triangle first. Align the ¼" line on the rotary ruler with the outside line, making sure the sandpaper tabs secure the ends.

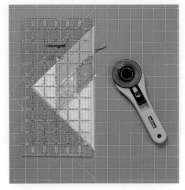

B. Next, trim the right-hand side of the triangle. Align the ¼" line on the rotary ruler with the outside line and trim.

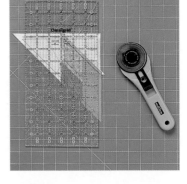

C. Lastly, trim the final side of the triangle. Align the ¼" line on the rotary ruler with the outside line and trim. Use the middle portion of the ruler as shown to hold the top tip in place while trimming. Do not remove the paper. That will come later.

Sewing Assembly-Line Fashion

IT IS MUCH more efficient to assembly-line sew the A sections first, and then sew the B sections. If this is your first paper-piecing experience, make one of each section first to see how it all works before you begin assembly-line sewing.

To sew the A sections in assembly-line fashion, pin all the #1 pieces in place and *trim them*. Place the foundations with the pinned pieces fabric side up next to you at the sewing machine. Position piece #2 and sew the first seam line. Pull the foundation away from the needle area, and then position and sew piece #2 on the next foundation. Continue until all the #2 pieces have been sewn to the four A sections.

Bring all the foundations to the ironing board. Lay them design side up and cut all the top threads. Flip the line of foundations fabric side up and clip all the threads. Press all the #2 pieces open.

Bring the stack of foundations to the cutting board and trim all the #2 pieces. Continue the assembly-line process with the remaining pieces.

Fixing Mistakes

IT'S EASY TO fix a mistake should you sew a piece incorrectly and need to remove it. Place a piece of Scotch brand removable tape on the seam line where you will be removing the piece. The tape will keep the paper intact. From the fabric side, lift the piece to be removed until the stitches at the end of the seam are visible. Lightly touch the stitches with an Olfa point cutter to cut them along the seam line. When the piece has been removed, resew the seam.

COMPLETING THE BLOCK

Joining Sections A and B

WHEN THE A and B sections are completed and trimmed, it is time to join them to make a quarter of the block. With section A facing you, place the A and B sections together, right sides facing. Place them long side down on a hard surface to align them. Hold the papers firmly and pin the right-angle corner.

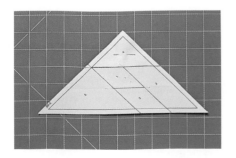

Walk your fingers along the inside points to align them and pin in place away from the seam line. Walk your fingers along the outside points to align them and pin in place. Place one more pin in the middle of the block.

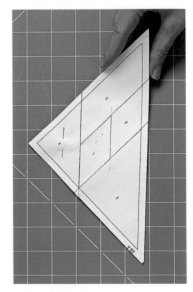

Trust me, you'll definitely want to follow these basting steps before you join the sections with a small stitch. Basting allows you to check that the seams really do match before you sew them, and it prevents the sections from shifting while you sew. Basting is well worth your time.

To baste, increase the stitch length to about four to five stitches per inch. With section A facing up, baste about one inch on the line at the beginning of the sections, at any matching points along the seam, and at the end of the sections.

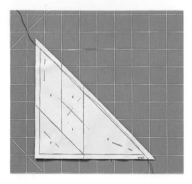

Remove the basted triangles from the sewing machine and check that you have basted on the seam line of section B. Open up the sections and check for a good match. If the match is good, sew on the line, using eighteen to twenty stitches per inch and starting from the center point of the star. If any of the matches are not good, clip the threads at just those seams and remove the basting. Adjust the seam, pin, and rebase until the match is good. With section B on top, open and press the seam allowances toward section B.

Adding Fabric Across Sections A and B

SOME OF THE star blocks have additional pieces of fabric that need to be sewn across sections A and B after the sections are joined. This is indicated on the block foundation and in the cutting list with an asterisk (*) following the number. When a block calls for this option, follow these steps:

1. Trim the last piece on each section ¼" from the next seam line as you normally would. In the following example, the #7 pieces were trimmed ¼" from line #8.

2. Trim the A and B sections ¼" from the outside line of the triangle.

3. Pin the A and B sections right sides together, making sure that the sewing lines meet for pieces to be sewn across both sections. Baste, check, and sew the diagonal seam.

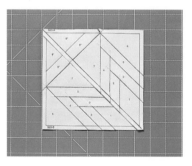

4. Continue foundation piecing across the joined sections. The following photograph shows piece #8 sewn in place across both sections and piece #9 in position ready to be flipped right sides together.

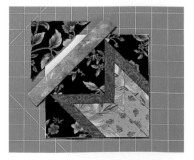

5. When the fabric piece(s) have been added, trim the added fabric pieces ¼" from the outside line.

Joining the Sections

JOIN THE FOUR quarters for one star block in the same way, clipping the dog ears that extend beyond the foundation. Place two quarters right sides together. Pin; baste at the beginning, at any matching points, and at the end; check for a good match.

Clip dog ears.

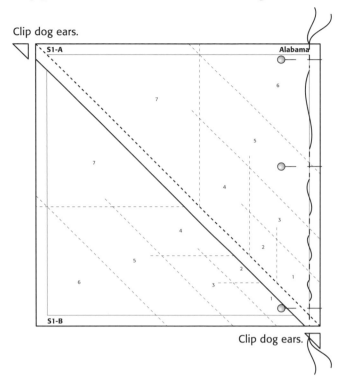

Clip dog ears.

When you are happy with the match, sew with a small stitch. Join the remaining two quarters. Press the seam allowance for both sets in the same direction. You now have two halves of a star.

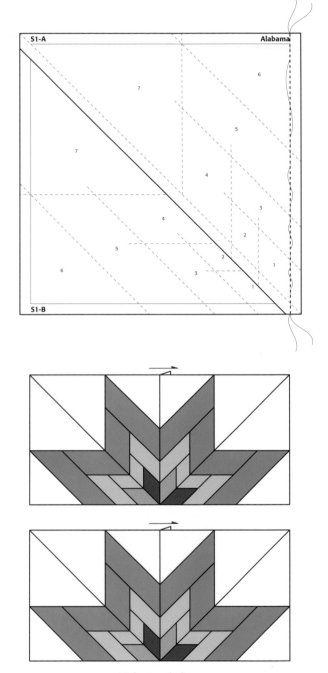

Make two halves.
Press seam allowances for both halves in the same direction.

With right sides facing, pin the two halves together. Baste at the beginning, at any matching points, and at the end. Check that you have a good match, and sew with a smaller stitch. I found that if I decreased the stitch length to twenty-five stitches per inch just at the center seam, it gave an even tighter match. Press the seam allowance down. If the center area is bulky and a bit higher than the remainder of the block, place a pressing cloth on top of this area when pressing.

Middle seam allowances will go in opposite directions.

Press seam allowance down.

Removing the Paper

Do NOT REMOVE the paper until the block is joined to other blocks or other straight-grain fabric pieces. The outside seam line acts as a sewing guide and the paper stabilizes the blocks. To remove the paper, begin in the center portion of the block and gently tug diagonally to pull the paper away from the stitching line. Use a small pair of tweezers to remove the paper pieces in the intersecting seams. This doesn't require a lot of attention, so it is a perfect activity when relaxing in the evening.

MIXING AND MATCHING SECTIONS

*T*HE FIFTY STAR blocks presented in this book are just the beginning of your creative opportunities. There are several more creative design avenues to explore that will produce an unbelievable number of new star blocks. One such design avenue is mixing and matching sections from different blocks. Since all the A sections are interchangeable and all the B sections are interchangeable, just think of the possibilities for new star blocks. The designs that result from this "what if" playing are amazing. I encourage you to play with the possibilities.

The small block-front drawings at the bottom of the pattern pages show how the star blocks will appear when they are completed. Use them to explore the possibilities of combining the A and B sections from different star designs. After you play with combining the different design options, you can play with coloring them in different ways. The following example shows the block-front drawings for the Alabama and Delaware star blocks. Look at the new star block created when you combine section A from the Alabama star and section B from the Delaware star.

I love to design patchwork, and when I think of the new designs created by combining the A and B sections, it boggles my mind. The following block combinations should get your creative juices flowing:

S1 Alabama

Section A

Section B

S1-A Alabama

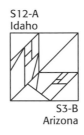

S8-B Delaware

S8 Delaware

Section A

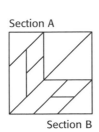

Section B

New star block

S3-A
Arizona

S12-B
Idaho

S12-A
Idaho

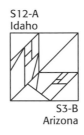

S3-B
Arizona

S29-A
New Hampshire

S40-B
South Carolina

S40-A
South Carolina

S29-B
New Hampshire

S5-A
California

S6-B
Colorado

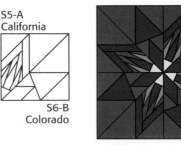

S38-A
Pennsylvania

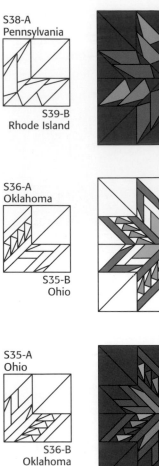

S39-B
Rhode Island

S18-A
Louisiana

S17-B
Kentucky

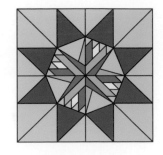

S36-A
Oklahoma

S35-B
Ohio

S33-A
North Carolina

S24-B
Mississippi

S35-A
Ohio

S36-B
Oklahoma

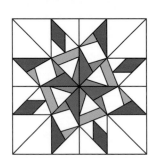

S3-A
Arizona

S29-B
New Hampshire

S26-A
Montana

S32-B
New York

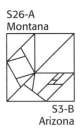

S26-A
Montana

S3-B
Arizona

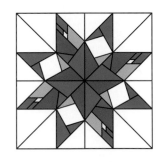

S2-A
Alaska

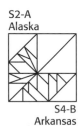

S4-B
Arkansas

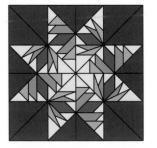

S9-A
Florida

S26-B
Montana

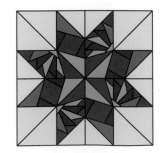

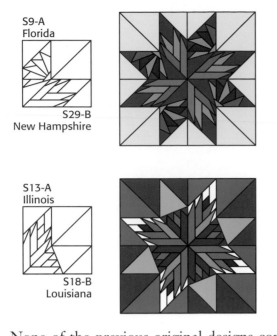

S9-A
Florida

S29-B
New Hampshire

S13-A
Illinois

S18-B
Louisiana

None of the previous original designs contain patchwork in the background areas of the star points. Star blocks 7, 11, 15, 23, 28, 37, 41, 42, 44, 45, and 50 do have patchwork in the background area. That doesn't mean you can't use these blocks; you just have to play with the designs. For example, section A from the Utah block would not match up with a B section from a different block because section A has patchwork in the background of the star (indicated by the shaded areas in the quarters shown below). You can, however, use section A from the Utah block if you eliminate the seam in the shaded area. Simply use a larger piece of fabric to cover the background triangle. In the completed stars below, the seam lines that were eliminated are not evident.

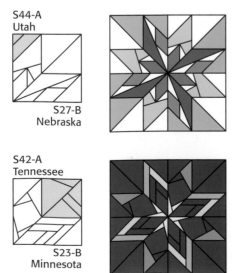

S44-A
Utah

S27-B
Nebraska

S42-A
Tennessee

S23-B
Minnesota

Another alternative to a pieced background area in one of the sections is to add a similar seam line to the other section that doesn't contain a pieced background area. In the following example, a seam line was added to section A of the Nebraska block so that it would align with a seam in section B of the Utah block. The small triangles in the middle of the block sides are the result of this addition.

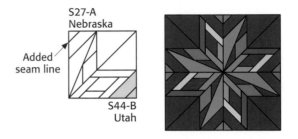

S27-A
Nebraska

Added
seam line

S44-B
Utah

Another avenue for mixing and matching is to use two quarters from one star block and two quarters from another block. Place the like quarters diagonally in the block to create even more star designs. The following new star blocks are examples of this design avenue.

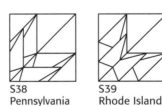

S38
Pennsylvania

S39
Rhode Island

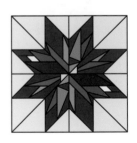

S12
Idaho

S25
Missouri

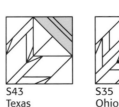

S43
Texas

S35
Ohio

Corner not pieced
in the Texas star.

FIFTY STAR BLOCKS

*G*ALLERY OF STARS" on pages 25–27 presents all fifty star blocks together. Use these pages to pick out the star you want to make or to visualize how sections from different stars might look together.

Following "Gallery of Stars" you'll find a photograph and a cutting list for each of the fifty 12" star blocks. Digital reproductions were made of the star block photography to show how four star blocks will look when joined. Several blocks have background patchwork elements that make secondary designs when joined, and these digital reproductions illustrate the design opportunities.

To indicate the time investment required, the number of pieces in each block is shown. A block made of forty pieces can be completed in about half the time of a block that contains eighty pieces. The following chart indicates the number of pieces in the star blocks. Don't shy away from the dramatic blocks with more pieces. They will take longer to make, but they are not more difficult to make, and are definitely worth the effort. A traditionally pieced feathered-star block design can contain 125 pieces, so the blocks with more pieces are quite reasonable.

Number of Pieces	Star Blocks
40	8, 16
48	6, 17, 27
56	1, 19, 20, 21, 26, 46, 49
60	7, 11, 28
64	12, 14, 23, 32, 37, 38, 39, 42, 44, 45, 47
68	25, 43
72	3, 30, 31, 33, 35, 50
80	10, 18, 24
88	34
96	5, 29
100	41
104	2, 4, 13
108	48
112	9, 15
120	40
128	22, 36

The cutting list provided with each star block is for making one block. I feel these cutting lists are worth their weight in gold. When I made a quilt using several different star blocks, it was so easy to cut the pieces, label them, and paper piece the A and B sections from the precut pieces. If you use different colors but the same fabric placements, follow the cutting list, substituting your color choice. If you decide to use a different fabric placement, determine the cut size of the piece needed for each number in the block sections and use your design to determine how many to cut.

The ◺ symbol in the cutting list indicates to

cut the squares once diagonally to create two half-square triangles (see pages 12–13). An asterisk (*) following a number indicates fabric pieces that are sewn after the A and B sections have been joined (see page 18). A dagger (†) following a number indicates that I chose to center a motif in the area (see page 9).

The foundation pages include a full-size paper-piecing foundation for each block. The foundations are the reverse of the finished block because you will be sewing from the back of the design. The sections are labeled with the number of the block and the section letter (A or B). The *S* pre-ceding the number stands for star. Make four copies each of section A and section B to make one star block. See page 7.

On the bottom of the foundation page is a block-front drawing of how the A and B sections will look from the fabric side. There are also two block-front drawings of the completed star block. These can be used in two different ways. You can use colored pencils to explore different color options and design avenues (see pages 10–11). You can also cut and paste together A and B sections from different star blocks to explore new star designs (see pages 20–23).

GALLERY OF STARS

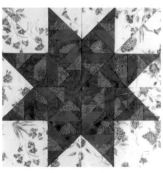

S1 ALABAMA

S2 ALASKA

S3 ARIZONA

S4 ARKANSAS

S5 CALIFORNIA

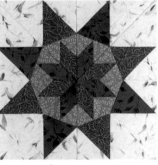

S6 COLORADO

S7 CONNECTICUT

S8 DELAWARE

S9 FLORIDA

S10 GEORGIA

S11 HAWAII

S12 IDAHO

S13 ILLINOIS

S14 INDIANA

S15 IOWA

S16 KANSAS

S17 KENTUCKY

S18 LOUISIANA

S19 MAINE

S20 MARYLAND

S21 MASSACHUSETTS

S22 MICHIGAN

S23 MINNESOTA

S24 MISSISSIPPI

S25 MISSOURI

S26 MONTANA

S27 NEBRASKA

S28 NEVADA

S29 NEW HAMPSHIRE

S30 NEW JERSEY

S31 NEW MEXICO

S32 NEW YORK

S33 NORTH CAROLINA

S34 NORTH DAKOTA

S35 OHIO

S36 OKLAHOMA

S37 OREGON

S38 PENNSYLVANIA

S39 RHODE ISLAND

S40 SOUTH CAROLINA

S41 SOUTH DAKOTA

S42 TENNESSEE

S43 TEXAS

S44 UTAH

S45 VERMONT

S46 VIRGINIA

S47 WASHINGTON

S48 WEST VIRGINIA

S49 WISCONSIN

S50 WYOMING

ALABAMA STAR

56 PIECES

The following cutting list is for one star block.

Fabric	No. of Pieces	Dimensions	Location Numbers	Section
Light teal	8	1½" x 2½"	1	A, B
Light pink	4	1½" x 2½"	2	A
	4	1½" x 3½"	3	B
Medium pink	4	1½" x 2½"	2	B
	4	1½" x 3½"	3	A
Medium-light teal	4	1¾" x 4"	4	A
	4	1¾" x 6"	5	B
Medium teal	4	1¾" x 4"	4	B
	4	1¾" x 6"	5	A
Black	4	3¾" x 3¾" ◺	6	A, B
	4	4¾" x 4¾" ◺	7	A, B

S1-A

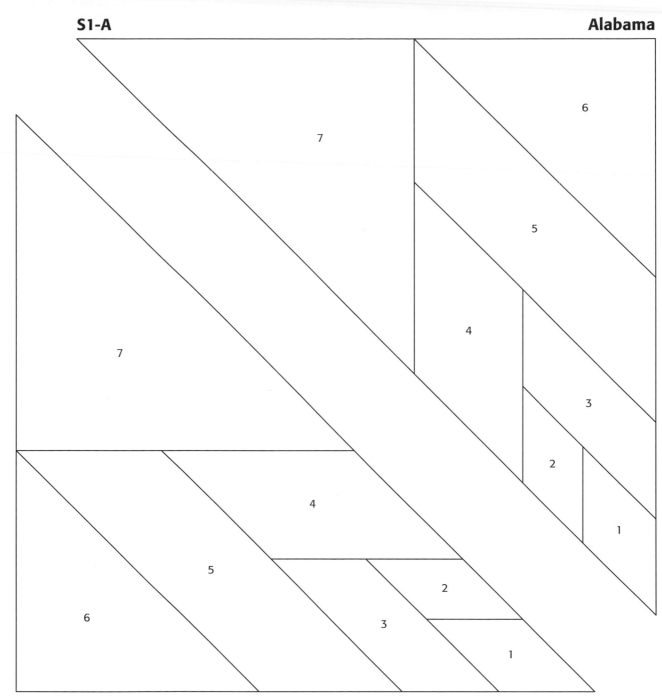

6

7

5

7

4

4

3

2

5

2

1

3

6

1

S1-B

A

B

Make 4.

Block-Front Drawings

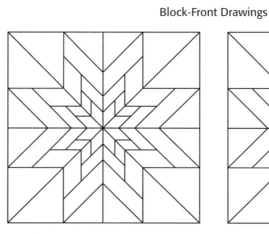

Alaska Star

104 PIECES

The following cutting list is for one star block.

Fabric	No. of Pieces	Dimensions	Location Numbers	Section
White	8	3" x 3" ◻	10, 11	A, B
	8	2¼" x 2¼" ◻	2, 3	A, B
	16	1½" x 2½"	6, 7	A, B
Medium blue #1	8	2" x 3½"	1†	A, B
Dark blue	16	1¼" x 3½"	4, 5	A, B
Medium blue #2	16	1¼" x 3½"	8, 9	A, B
Navy	4	3¾" x 3¾" ◻	12	A, B
	4	4¾" x 4¾" ◻	13	A, B

† The same motif is centered in area #1. See page 9.

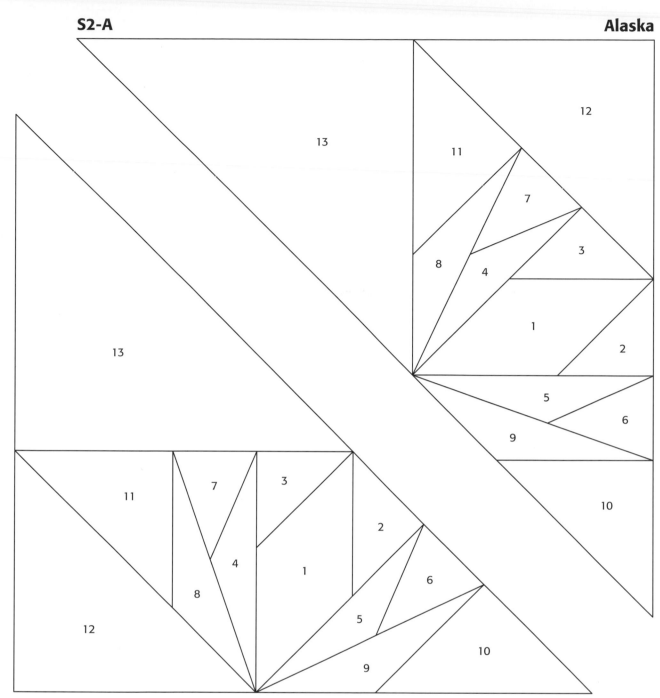

S2-B

Make 4.

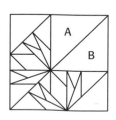

Block-Front Drawings

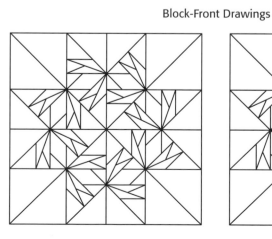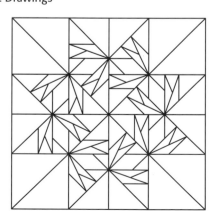

Arizona Star

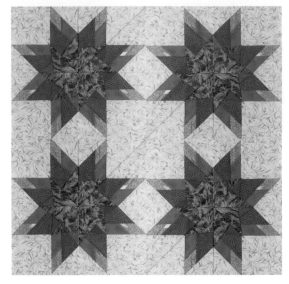

72 PIECES

The following cutting list is for one star block.

Fabric	No. of Pieces	Dimensions	Location Numbers	Section
Gold	8	1" x 1½"	1	A, B
Light blue	8	1" x 2"	2	A, B
	8	1¼" x 3"	3	A, B
Light peach	8	2¼" x 3"	4	A, B
Medium peach	8	2¼" x 4"	5	A, B
Dark green	8	1½" x 3"	6	A, B
Light green	8	2¾" x 4"	7	A, B
White print	4	3¾" x 3¾" ◻	8	A, B
	4	4¾" x 4¾" ◻	9	A, B

S3-A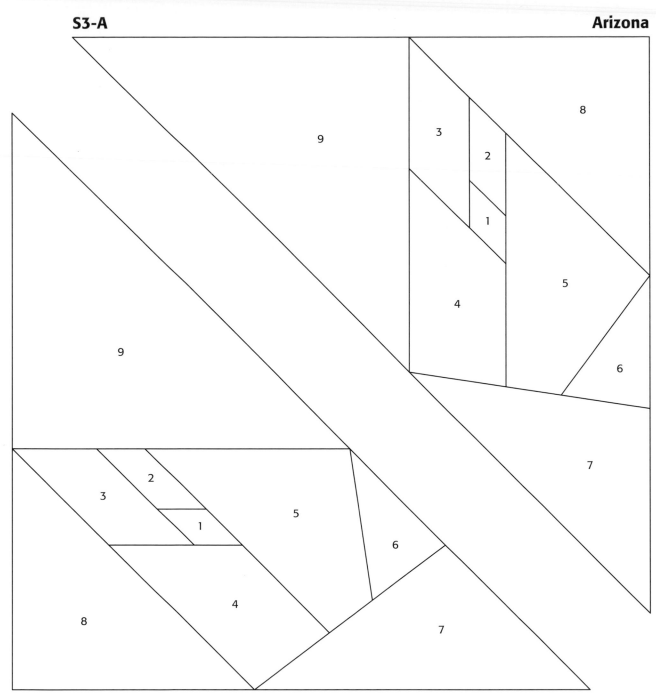

S3-B

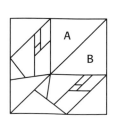

Make 4.

Block-Front Drawings

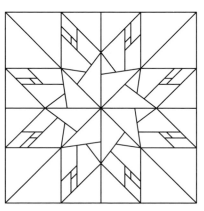 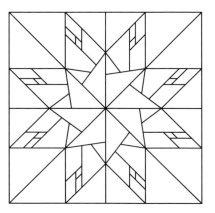

ARKANSAS STAR

104 PIECES

The following cutting list is for one star block.

Fabric	No. of Pieces	Dimensions	Location Numbers	Section
Pink print	8	1¾" x 3½"	1	A, B
Pink	16	1½" x 3½"	4, 5	A, B
Light purple	8	2½" x 2½" ◻	8, 9	A, B
Dark green	16	2½" x 2½" ◻	2, 3, 10, 11	A, B
	8	2" x 2" ◻	6, 7	A, B
White print	4	3¾" x 3¾" ◻	12	A, B
	4	4¾" x 4¾" ◻	13	A, B

S4-A

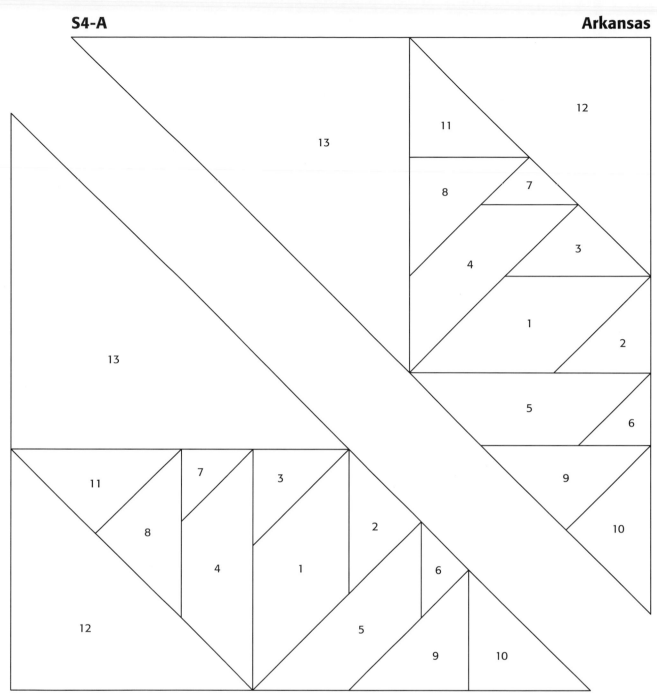

13

12

11

8   7

4   3

1

2

5   6

9

10

13

11   7   3

8   2

4   1

12   5   6

9   10

S4-B

Block-Front Drawings

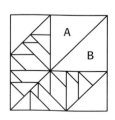

A
B

Make 4.

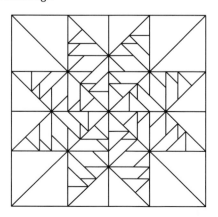

35

CALIFORNIA STAR

96 PIECES

The following cutting list is for one star block.

Fabric	No. of Pieces	Dimensions	Location Numbers	Section
Focal print	8	2" x 4"	1†	A, B
Peach	16	1¼" x 3½"	4, 5	A, B
Rust stripe	8	1½" x 5"	9	A
			8	B
Rust	8	1½" x 5"	8	A
			9	B
Black solid	32	1" x 4"	2, 3, 6, 7	A, B
Black print	8	2" x 2"	10	A, B
	4	3¾" x 3¾" ◻	11	A, B
	4	4¾" x 4¾" ◻	12	A, B

† The same motif is centered in area #1. See page 9.

S5-A

California

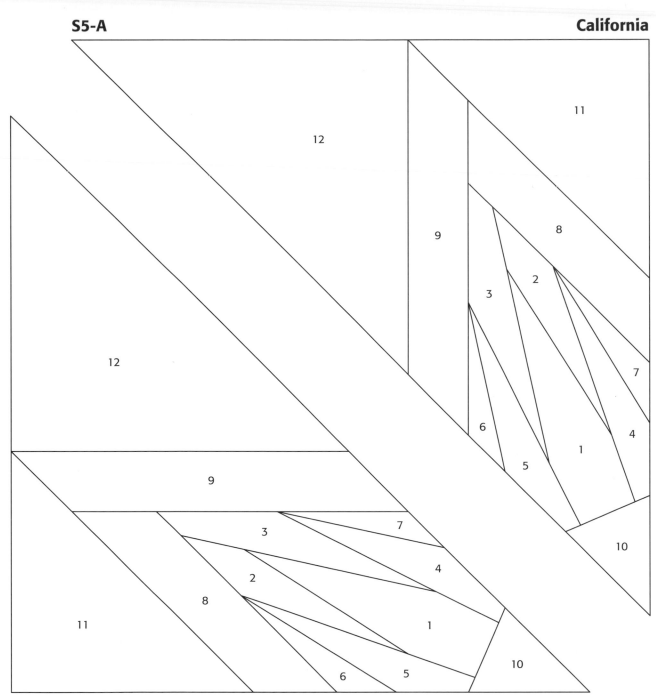

12

11

12

9

8

3

2

7

6

1

4

5

10

9

7

3

4

2

1

8

11

6

5

10

S5-B

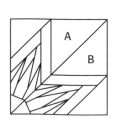

Make 4.

Block-Front Drawings

COLORADO STAR

48 PIECES

The following cutting list is for one star block.

Fabric	No. of Pieces	Dimensions	Location Numbers	Section
Pink	4	2" x 4"	1	A
	4	3½" x 4"	4	A
Dark blue	4	2" x 4"	1	B
	4	3½" x 4"	4	B
Medium blue	16	2" x 3"	2, 3	A, B
White print	4	3¾" x 3¾" ◻	5	A, B
	4	4¾" x 4¾" ◻	6	A, B

38

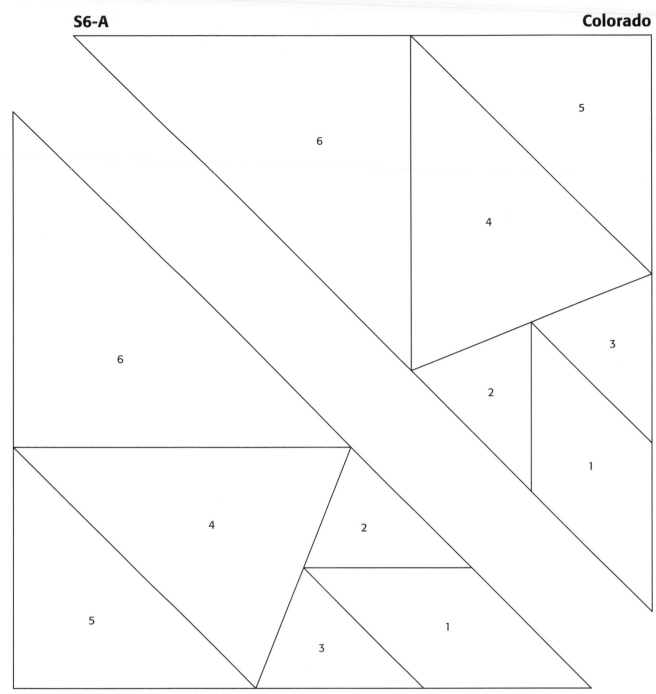

S6-B

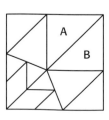

Make 4.

Block-Front Drawings

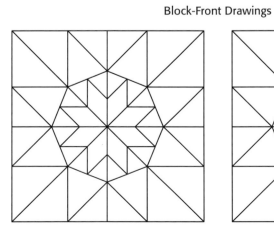

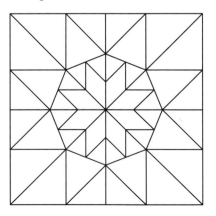

CONNECTICUT STAR

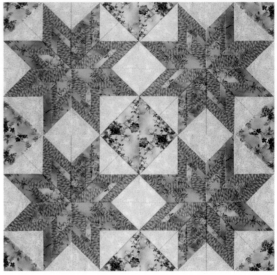

60 PIECES

The following cutting list is for one star block.

Fabric	No. of Pieces	Dimensions	Location Numbers	Section
Green	4	2" x 4"	1	B
	8	1" x 4"	2, 3	A
	4	1½" x 4½"	4	B
	4	1½" x 6"	5	B
Purple	4	2" x 4"	1	A
	8	1" x 4"	2, 3	B
	4	1½" x 4½"	4	A
	4	1½" x 6"	5	A
Floral	2	4¾" x 4¾" ◨	8*	A, B
Beige	8	3¾" x 3¾" ◨	6, 7	A, B

*Add these pieces after sections A and B are joined. See page 18.

40

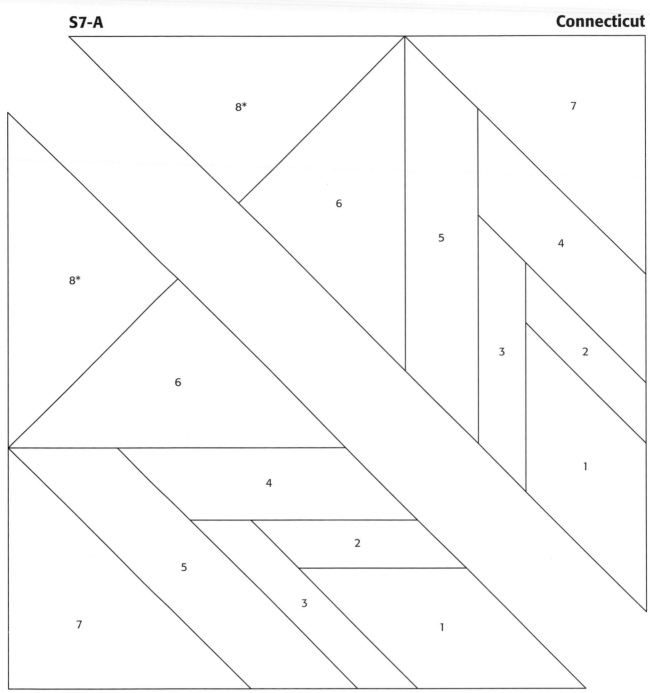

8*

7

6

5

4

3

2

8*

6

4

2

5

3

7

1

1

S7-B

Block-Front Drawings

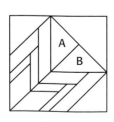

Make 4.

DELAWARE STAR

40 PIECES

The following cutting list is for one star block.

Fabric	No. of Pieces	Dimensions	Location Numbers	Section
Medium blue	8	2" x 4"	1	A, B
Pink	8	2" x 4"	2	A, B
Green	8	2" x 6"	3	A, B
Floral	4	3¾" x 3¾" ◻	4	A, B
	4	4¾" x 4¾" ◻	5	A, B

S8-A   **Delaware**

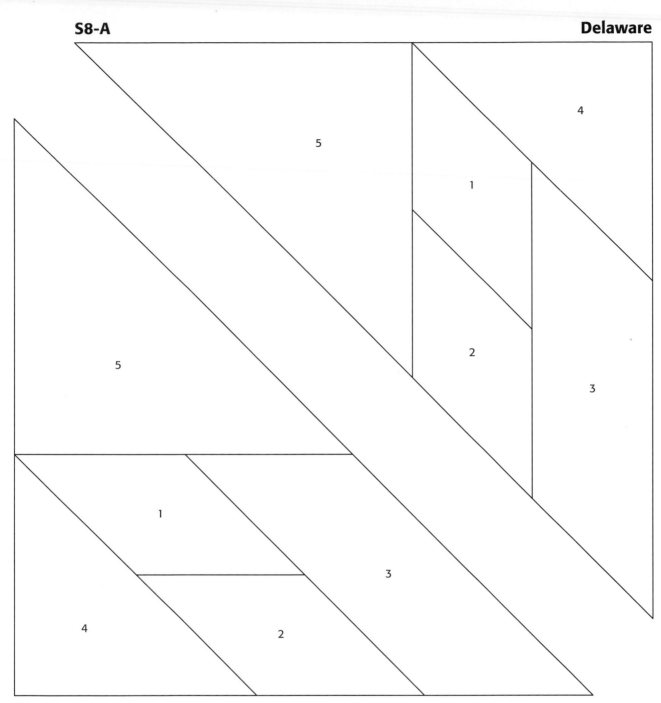

S8-B

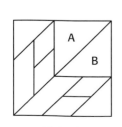

Make 4.

Block-Front Drawings

43

FLORIDA STAR

112 PIECES

The following cutting list is for one star block.

Fabric	No. of Pieces	Dimensions	Location Numbers	Section
Rust #1	8	1¼" x 3"	1	A, B
Rust #2	8	1¼" x 3"	3	A, B
Rust #3	8	1¼" x 3"	5	A, B
Rust #4	8	1¼" x 3"	7	A, B
Rust #5	8	1¼" x 3"	9	A, B
Black	32	1½" x 2¼"	2, 4, 6, 8	A, B
	8	2" x 2¼"	10	A, B
	8	2½" x 4½"	12	A, B
Green	8	1¼" x 2½"	11	A, B
Beige	4	3¾" x 3¾" ◻	13	A, B
	4	4¾" x 4¾" ◻	14	A, B

44

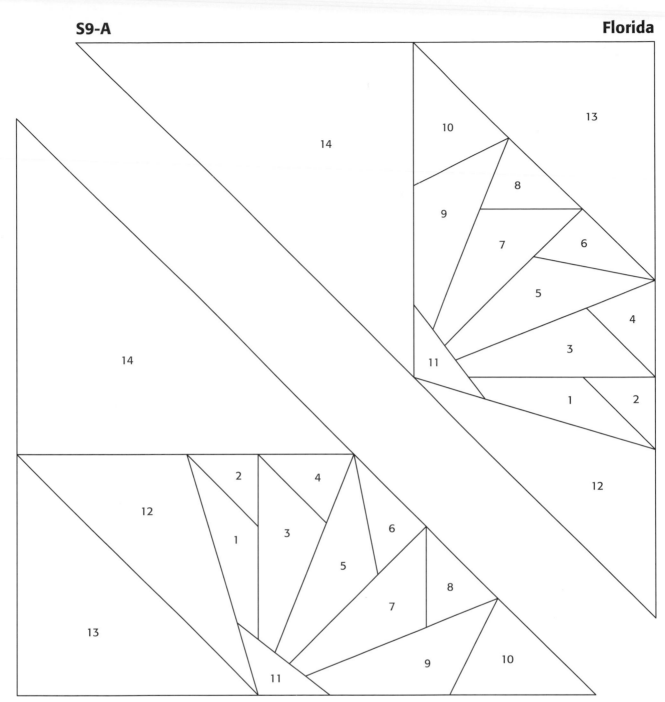

S9-B

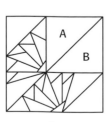

Make 4.

Block-Front Drawings

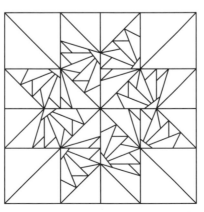
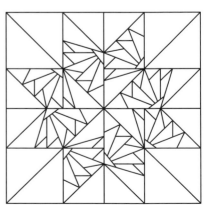

GEORGIA STAR

80 PIECES

The following cutting list is for one star block.

Fabric	No. of Pieces	Dimensions	Location Numbers	Section
Yellow	8	1½" x 2¾"	1	A, B
Medium green	8	1½" x 5"	4	A, B
Dark green	8	1½" x 6"	5	A, B
Light blue	8	2" x 2½"	2	A, B
	8	2" x 3"	3	A, B
	16	1¼" x 3"	6, 7	A, B
	8	2½" x 2½"	8	A, B
White print	4	3¾" x 3¾" ◱	9	A, B
	4	4¾" x 4¾" ◱	10	A, B

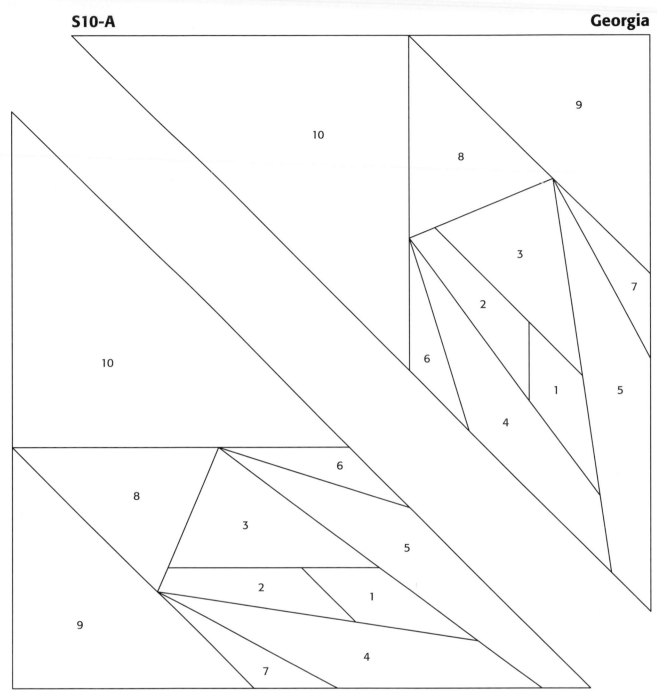

S10-B

Block-Front Drawings

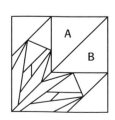

Make 4.

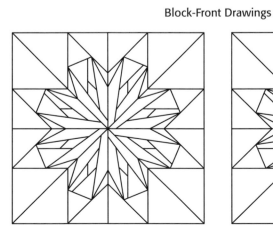

HAWAII STAR

60 PIECES

The following cutting list is for one star block.

Fabric	No. of Pieces	Dimensions	Location Numbers	Section
White print	4	1¼" x 2¾"	2	B
	4	1¼" x 4"	3	B
	4	2" x 4½"	1	A
	4	2" x 6½"	8*	A, B
	4	1½" x 4"	10*	A, B
Dark teal	4	1½" x 3"	1	B
Medium green	4	1½" x 4"	4	B
Light teal	4	1¾" x 5½"	5	B
Aqua	4	1¾" x 5½"	3	A
Light green	4	1¾" x 4"	2	A
Teal leaf print	8	3¾" x 3¾" �	4, 5	A
			6, 7	B
Royal blue	4	2" x 5½"	9*	A, B

*Add these pieces after sections A and B are joined. See page 18.

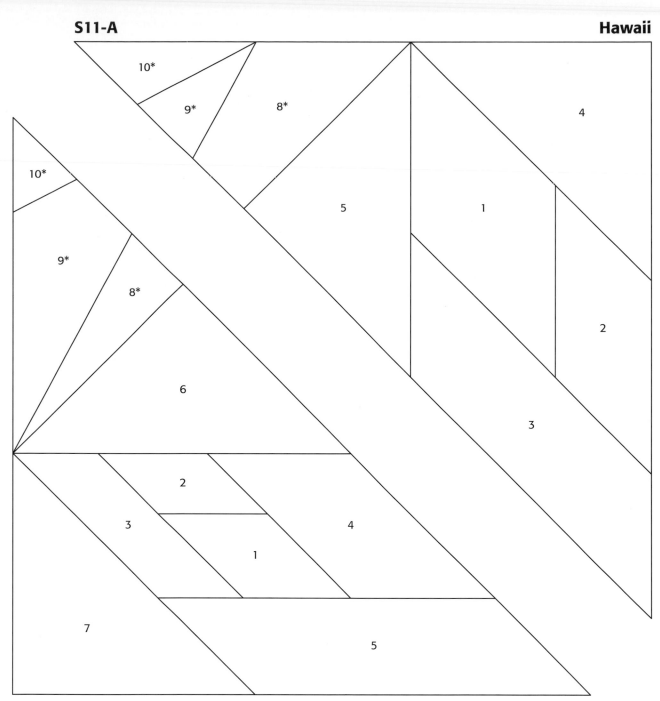

S11-B

Block-Front Drawings

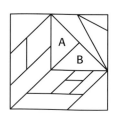

Make 4.

IDAHO STAR

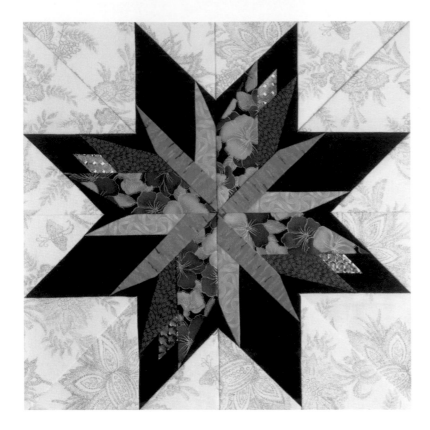

64 PIECES

The following cutting list is for one star block.

Fabric	No. of Pieces	Dimensions	Location Numbers	Section
Gold	4	1¼" x 2½"	1	A
Black	4	1¼" x 2½"	2	A
	12	1¼" x 3½"	3, 6, 7	A
	8	1" x 3"	4, 5	B
	4	2½" x 5½"	1	B
Medium-light green	4	1¼" x 4"	2	B
Medium green	4	1¼" x 5"	3	B
Purple	4	2" x 4"	4	A
Floral	4	2" x 6"	5	A
White print	4	3¾" x 3¾" ◻	9	A
			6	B
	4	4¾" x 4¾" ◻	8	A
			7	B

S12-A

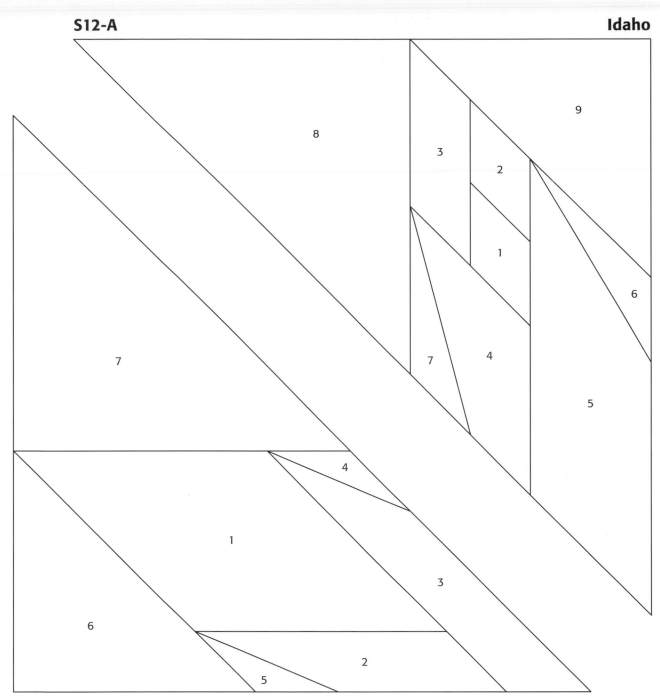

8

9

3

2

1

6

7

4

5

S12-B

7

4

1

3

6

2

5

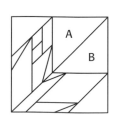

A

B

Make 4.

Block-Front Drawings

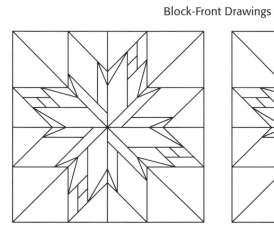

ILLINOIS STAR

104 PIECES

The following cutting list is for one star block.

Fabric	No. of Pieces	Dimensions	Location Numbers	Section
Dark red	8	1¼" x 2¼"	1	A, B
Light red	8	1¼" x 3"	4	A, B
Medium red	8	1¼" x 4"	5	A, B
White print	8	1¼" x 2¼"	2	A, B
	8	1¼" x 3½"	3	A, B
	32	1" x 2½"	6, 7, 10, 11	A, B
Medium green	8	1¼" x 4"	8	A, B
Dark green #1	8	1¼" x 5"	9	A, B
Dark green #2	4	3¾" x 3¾" ◳	12	A, B
	4	4¾" x 4¾" ◳	13	A, B

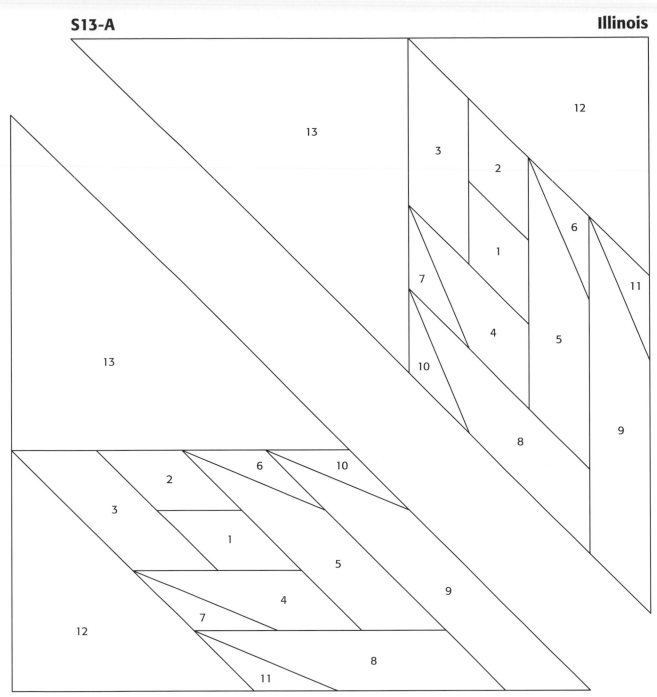

S13-A

Illinois

13

12

3

2

1

6

7

11

10

4

5

8

9

13

S13-B

2

3

6

10

1

5

4

7

9

12

8

11

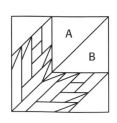

Make 4.

Block-Front Drawings

ℐNDIANA 𝒮TAR

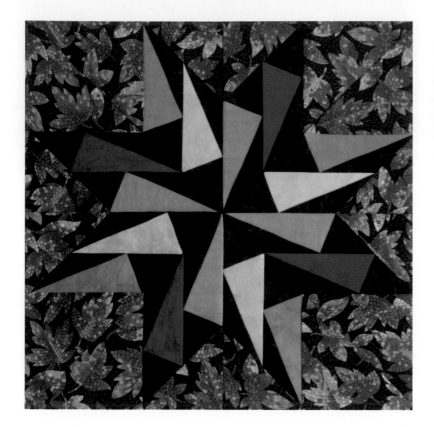

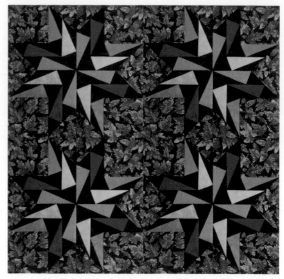

64 PIECES

The following cutting list is for one star block.

Fabric	No. of Pieces	Dimensions	Location Numbers	Section
Dark blue	4	2" x 4½"	1	B
Light blue	4	2" x 4½"	4	B
Dark pink	4	2" x 4½"	4	A
Light pink	4	2" x 4½"	1	A
Black	16	2¼" x 2¼"	2, 5	A, B
	16	1¼" x 4"	6, 3	A, B
Leaf print	4	3¾" x 3¾" ◰	7	A, B
	4	4¾" x 4¾" ⊠	8	A, B

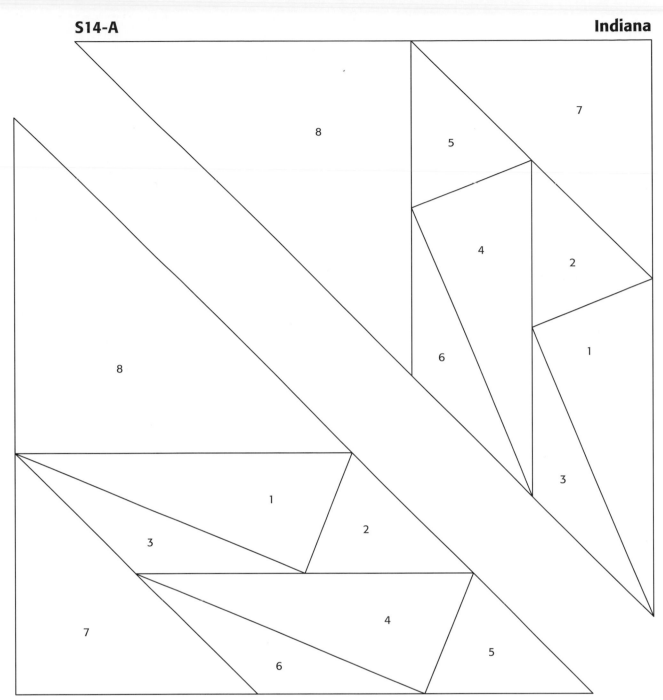

8

7

5

4

2

8

6

1

1

3

2

3

7

4

6

5

S14-B

Block-Front Drawings

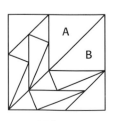

A

B

Make 4.

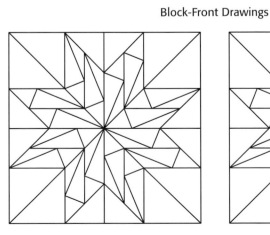

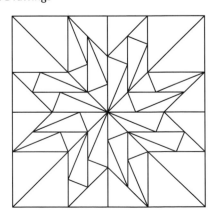

IOWA STAR

112 PIECES

The following cutting list is for one star block.

Fabric	No. of Pieces	Dimensions	Location Numbers	Section
Blue	8	1¼" x 2"	2	A, B
Purple	8	2½" x 2½" ◻	11, 13	A, B
	8	1¼" x 3"	3	A, B
Light peach	8	1¼" x 3½"	4	A, B
Dark peach	8	1¼" x 4"	5	A, B
Light green	4	1¼" x 4"	8	B
	4	1¼" x 5"	9	A
Medium green	4	1¼" x 5"	9	B
	4	1¼" x 4	8	A
Dark green	8	1¼" x 2"	1	A, B
	16	1" x 2½"	6, 7	A, B
	4	2½" x 2½" ◻	14	A, B
Floral	8	1½" x 5"	10	A, B
	8	3" x 4½"	12	A, B

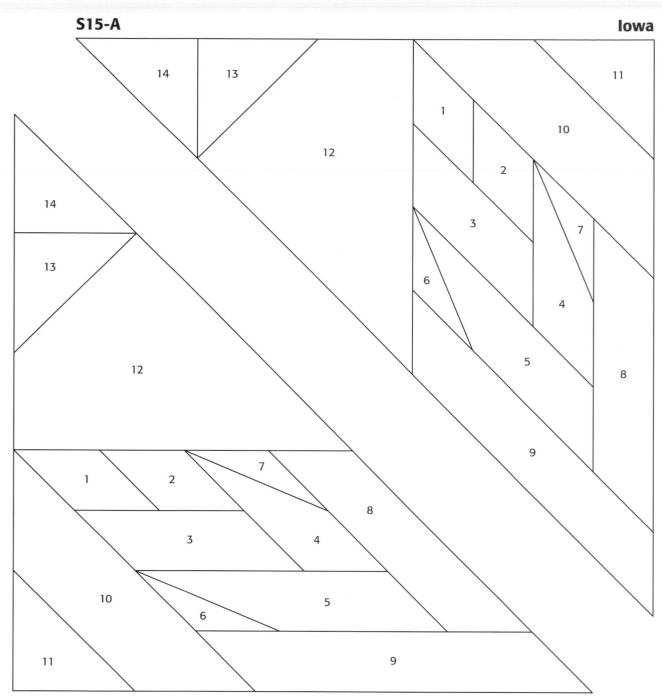

14   13

12

11

1

10

2

3   7

6

4

5

8

9

14

13

12

1   2   7

3   4   8

10

6   5

11   9

S15-B

Block-Front Drawings

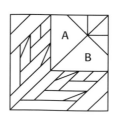

Make 4.

KANSAS STAR

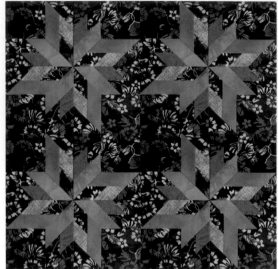

40 PIECES

The following cutting list is for one star block.

Fabric	No. of Pieces	Dimensions	Location Numbers	Section
Blue solid	4	2" x 6"	3	A
Purple print	4	2" x 3¾"	2	A
Purple solid	4	2" x 6"	3	B
Blue print	4	2" x 3¾"	2	B
Black print	8	2" x 3¾"	1	A, B
	4	3¾" x 3¾" ◻	4	A, B
	4	4¾" x 4¾" ◻	5	A, B

S16-A

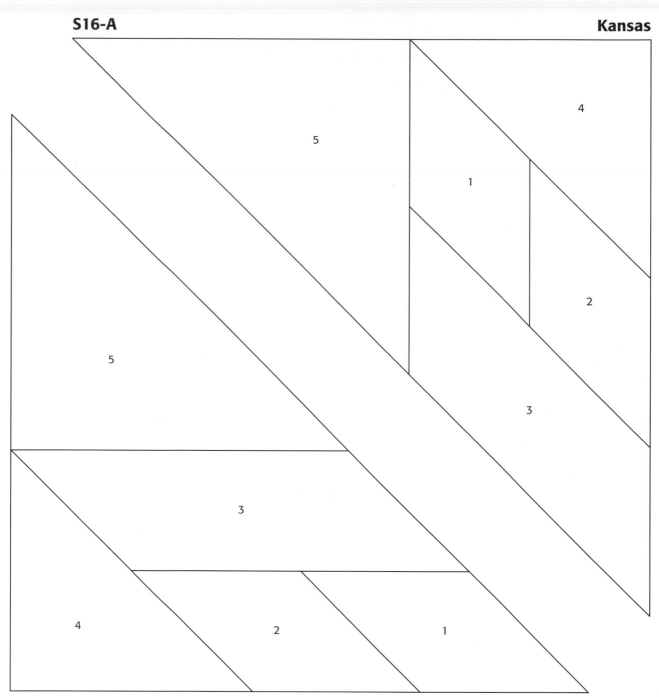

S16-B

Block-Front Drawings

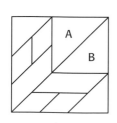

Make 4.

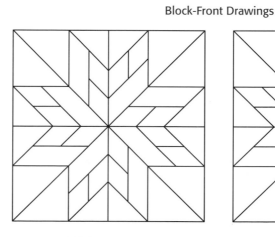

KENTUCKY STAR

48 PIECES

The following cutting list is for one star block.

Fabric	No. of Pieces	Dimensions	Location Numbers	Section
Fuchsia batik	8	3½" x 4"	1	A, B
Light fuchsia	4	1½" x 3½"	3	A
Medium fuchsia	4	1½" x 4½"	4	A
Dark purple	4	1½" x 3½"	3	B
Dark fuchsia	4	1½" x 4½"	4	B
Black	8	2½" x 3½"	2	A, B
	4	3¾" x 3¾" ◨	5	A, B
	4	4¾" x 4¾" ◨	6	A, B

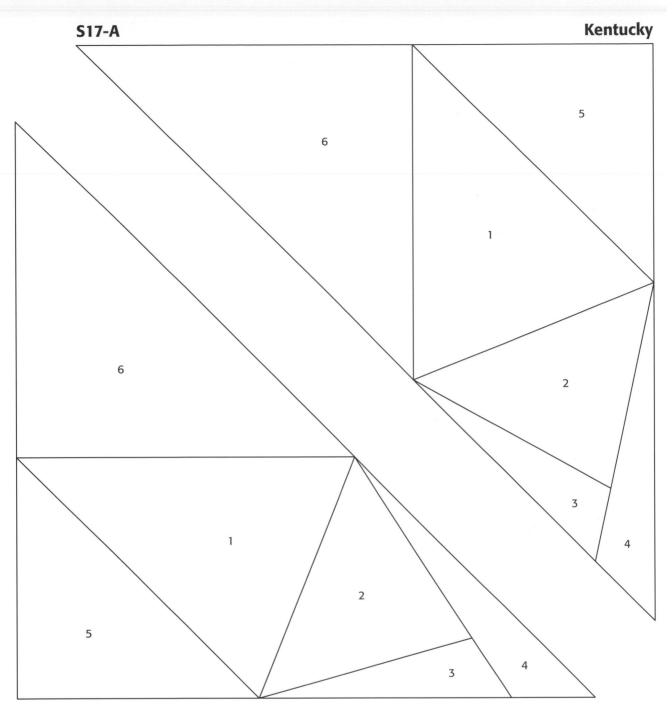

S17-B

Make 4.

Block-Front Drawings

LOUISIANA STAR

80 PIECES

The following cutting list is for one star block.

Fabric	No. of Pieces	Dimensions	Location Numbers	Section
Green floral	8	3½" x 4"	8	A, B
Red #1	8	1¼" x 2"	1	A, B
Red #2	8	1¼" x 3"	4	A, B
Red #3	8	1¼" x 4"	5	A, B
Black	32	1¼" x 1¾"	2, 3, 6, 7	A, B
	4	3¾" x 3¾" �«	9	A, B
	4	4¾" x 4¾" �«	10	A, B

62

S18-A

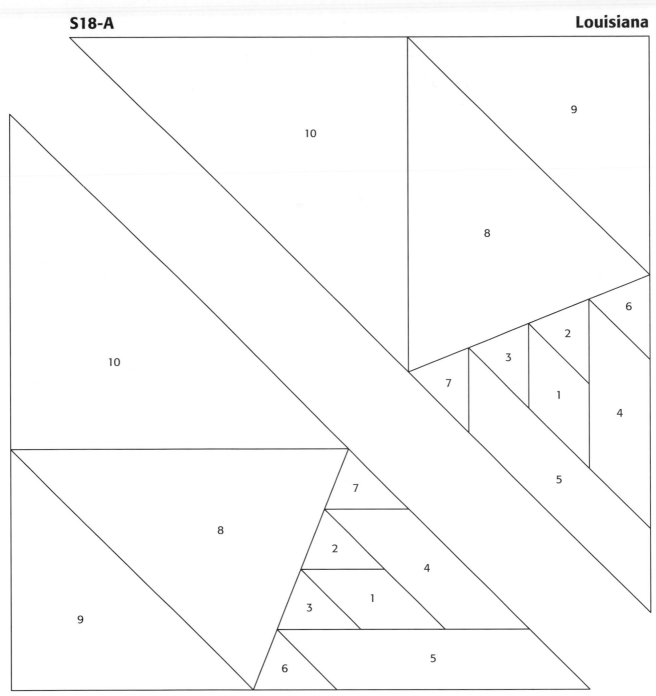

9

10

8

6

2

3

7

1

4

5

S18-B

10

8

7

2

4

3

1

5

9

6

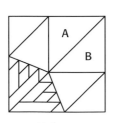

A

B

Make 4.

Block-Front Drawings

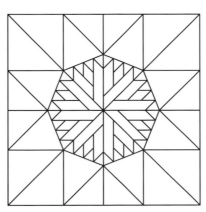

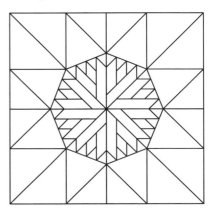

MAINE STAR

56 PIECES

The following cutting list is for one star block.

Fabric	No. of Pieces	Dimensions	Location Numbers	Section
Assorted solid colors	16	1¼" x 3"	2, 3	A, B
	16	1¼" x 5"	4, 5	A, B
Black	8	2" x 4"	1	A, B
	4	3¾" x 3¾" ◻	6	A, B
	4	4¾" x 4¾" ◻	7	A, B

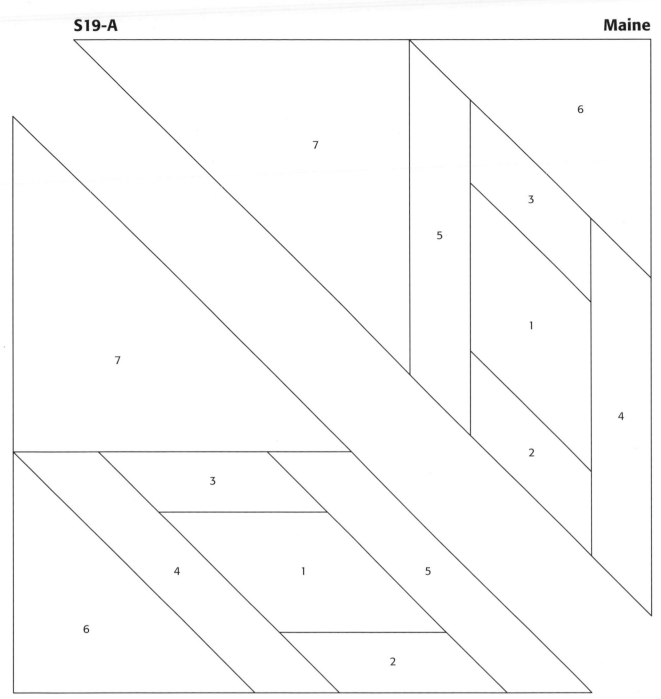

S19-B

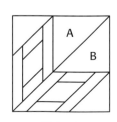

Make 4.

Block-Front Drawings

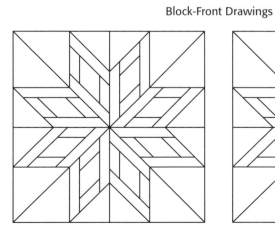

MARYLAND STAR

56 PIECES

The following cutting list is for one star block.

Fabric	No. of Pieces	Dimensions	Location Numbers	Section
White	8	2" x 4"	1	A, B
	16	1¼" x 3¾"	4, 5	A, B
Purple	4	2" x 3¾"	2	B
Medium blue	4	2" x 5½"	3	B
Green	4	2" x 3¾"	2	A
Floral	4	2" x 5½"	3	A
Dark blue	4	3¾" x 3¾" 	6	A, B
	4	4¾" x 4¾"	7	A, B

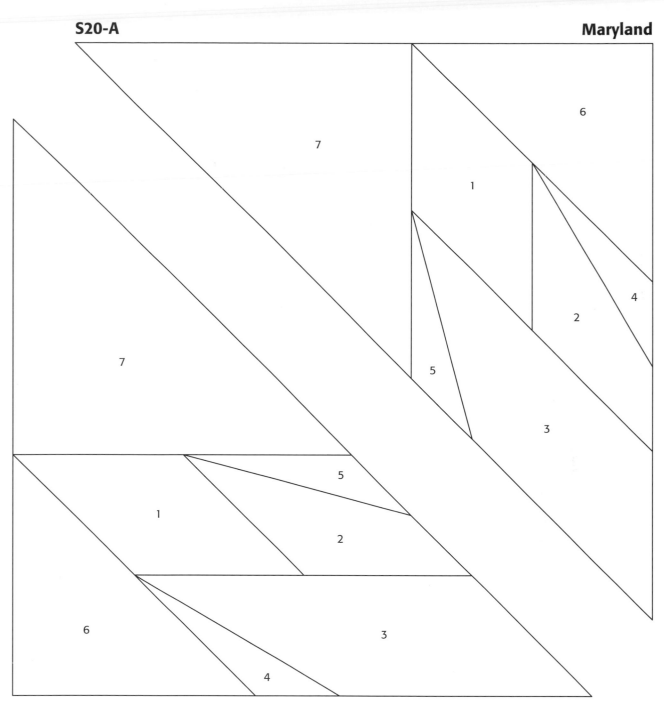

S20-B

Block-Front Drawings

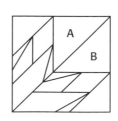

Make 4.

MASSACHUSETTS STAR

56 PIECES

The following cutting list is for one star block.

Fabric	No. of Pieces	Dimensions	Location Numbers	Section
Dark green	8	2¾" x 3"	3	A, B
Light blue	16	1¼" x 4"	2, 4	A, B
Medium blue	8	1¼" x 5"	5	A, B
Floral	8	2½" x 2½"	1	A, B
	4	3¾" x 3¾" ◻	6	A, B
	4	4¾" x 4¾" ◻	7	A, B

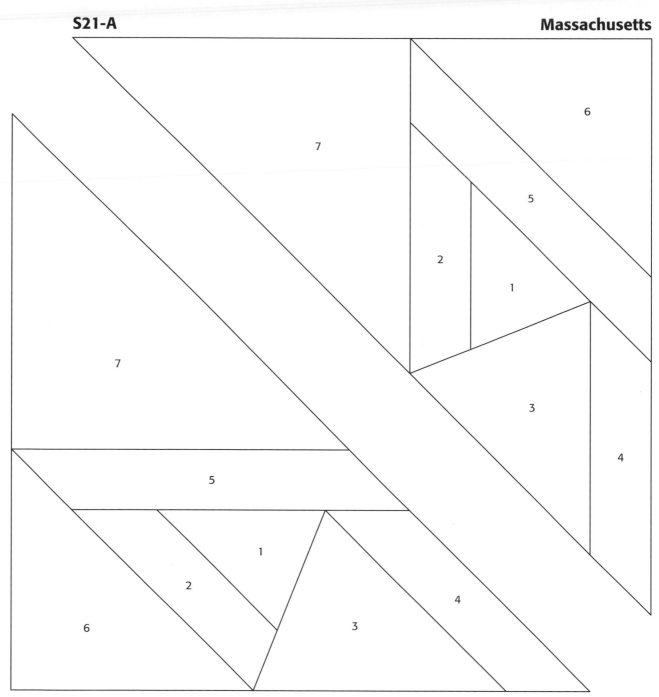

S21-B

Block-Front Drawings

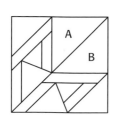

Make 4.

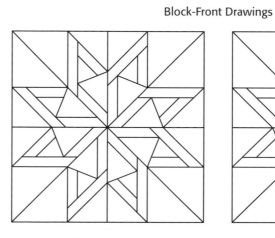

Michigan Star

128 PIECES

The following cutting list is for one star block.

Fabric	No. of Pieces	Dimensions	Location Numbers	Section
Light fuchsia	8	1½" x 5"	14	A, B
Dark fuchsia	8	1½" x 5"	13	A, B
Pink	8	1¼" x 2½"	1	A, B
Light blue	8	1¼" x 2½"	4	A, B
Medium blue	8	1¼" x 2½"	7	A, B
Purple	8	1¼" x 2½"	10	A, B
Black	32	1¼" x 2½"	3, 5, 8, 11	A, B
	32	1½" x 1½"	2, 6, 9, 12	A, B
	4	3¾" x 3¾" ◸	15	A, B
	4	4¾" x 4¾" ◸	16	A, B

70

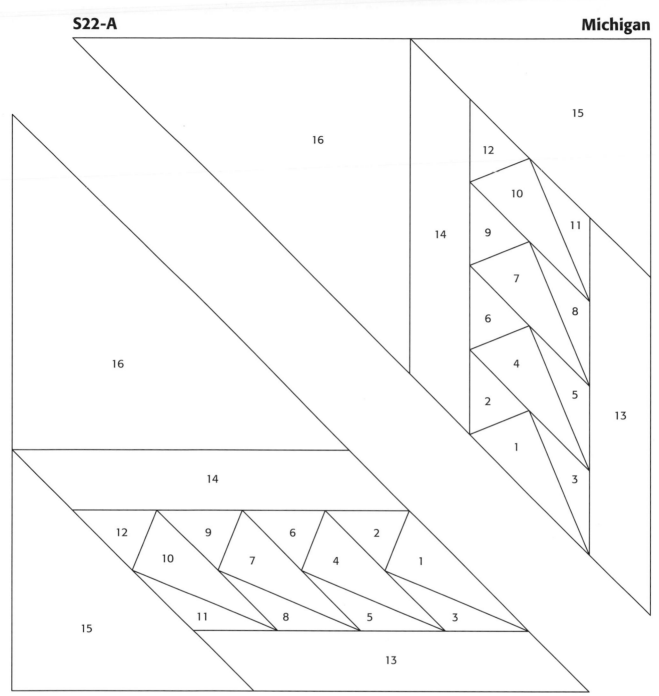

S22-B

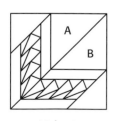

Make 4.

Block-Front Drawings

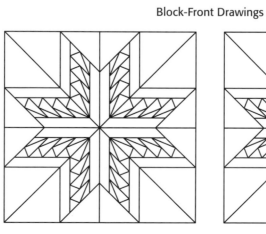

STAR BLOCK 23
Minnesota Star

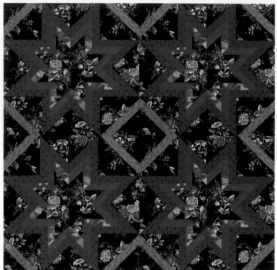

64 PIECES

The following cutting list is for one star block.

Fabric	No. of Pieces	Dimensions	Location Numbers	Section
Black floral	8	2½" x 4"	1	A, B
	10	3¾" x 3¾" ◻	6, 7	A, B
			9*	A, B
Light red	8	1½" x 3½"	2	A, B
Medium red	8	1½" x 4½"	3	A, B
Dark red	8	1½" x 4½"	4	A, B
	8	1½" x 5½"	5	A, B
Green	4	1½" x 6"	8*	A, B

*Add these pieces after sections A and B are joined. See page 18.

72

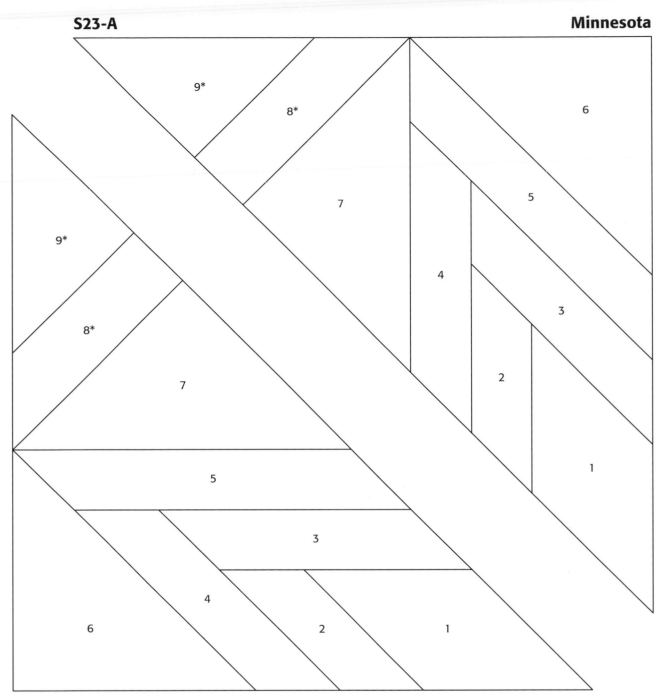

S23-B

Block-Front Drawings

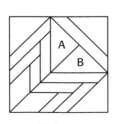

Make 4.

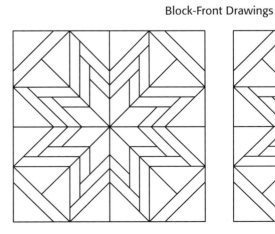

MISSISSIPPI STAR

80 PIECES

The following cutting list is for one star block.

Fabric	No. of Pieces	Dimensions	Location Numbers	Section
White	8	1¼" x 2¼"	2	A, B
	16	1¼" x 3"	4, 5	A, B
	8	2" x 2¼"	6	A, B
Medium teal	8	1¼" x 4"	7	A, B
Dark teal	8	1¼" x 5"	8	A, B
Medium purple	8	1½" x 3"	1	A, B
Dark purple	8	2" x 3½"	3	A, B
Floral	4	3¾" x 3¾" ◲	9	A, B
	4	4¾" x 4¾" ◲	10	A, B

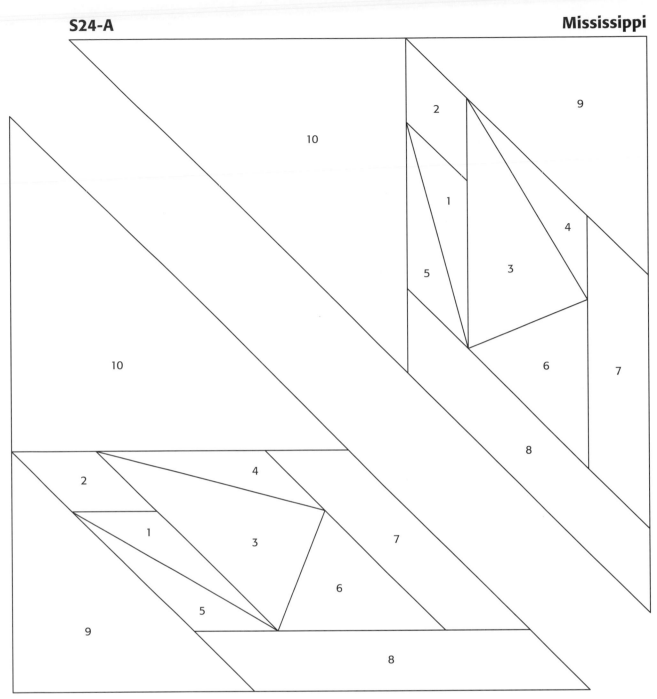

S24-B

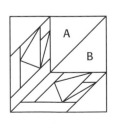

Make 4.

Block-Front Drawings

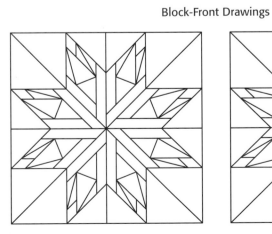

MISSOURI STAR

68 PIECES

The following cutting list is for one star block.

Fabric	No. of Pieces	Dimensions	Location Numbers	Section
Navy	8	2" x 4"	1	A, B
	8	1½" x 5"	4, 5	B
	8	1½" x 4"	4, 5	A
	4	1½" x 2"	6	A
Medium-light green	4	1½" x 3"	2	B
	4	1½" x 2½"	7	A
Medium green	4	1½" x 4¾"	3	B
Light green	2	2¼" x 2¼" ◻	6	B
Medium blue	4	1¾" x 4"	2	A
Blue/purple print	4	2" x 4¼"	3	A
Light blue print	4	3¾" x 3¾" ◻	8	A
			7	B
	4	4¾" x 4¾" ◻	9	A
			8	B

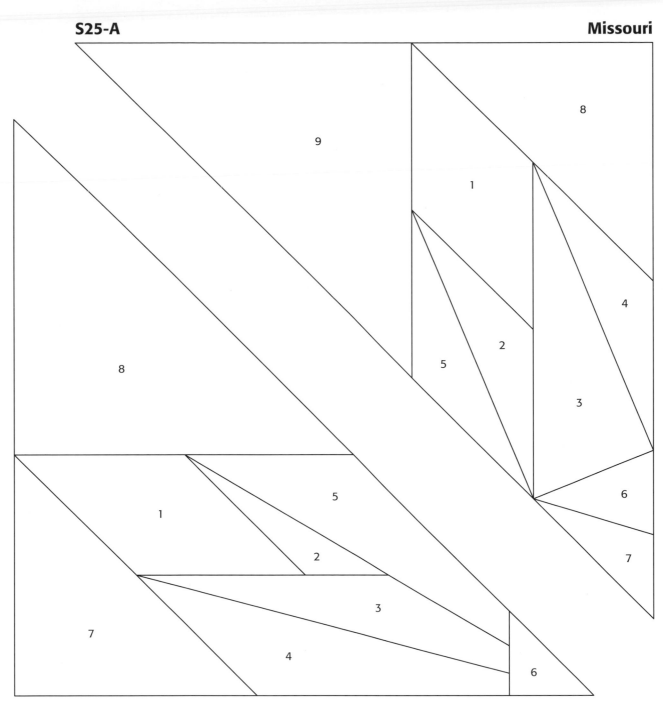

S25-B

Block-Front Drawings

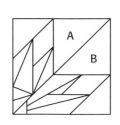

Make 4.

MONTANA STAR

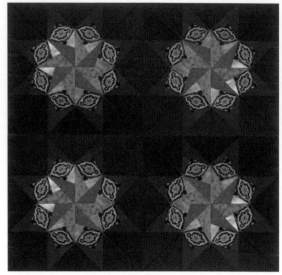

56 PIECES

The following cutting list is for one star block.

Fabric	No. of Pieces	Dimensions	Location Numbers	Section
Large-scale print	8	3" x 4"	1†	A, B
Red #1	8	1½" x 3"	2	A, B
Copper	8	1½" x 3"	3	A, B
Light brown	4	2½" x 4½"	4	A
Medium brown	4	2½" x 4½"	4	B
Red #2	8	2½" x 4½"	5	A, B
Dark brown	4	3¾" x 3¾" ◻	6	A, B
	4	4¾" x 4¾" ◻	7	A, B

† The same motif is centered in area #1. See page 9.

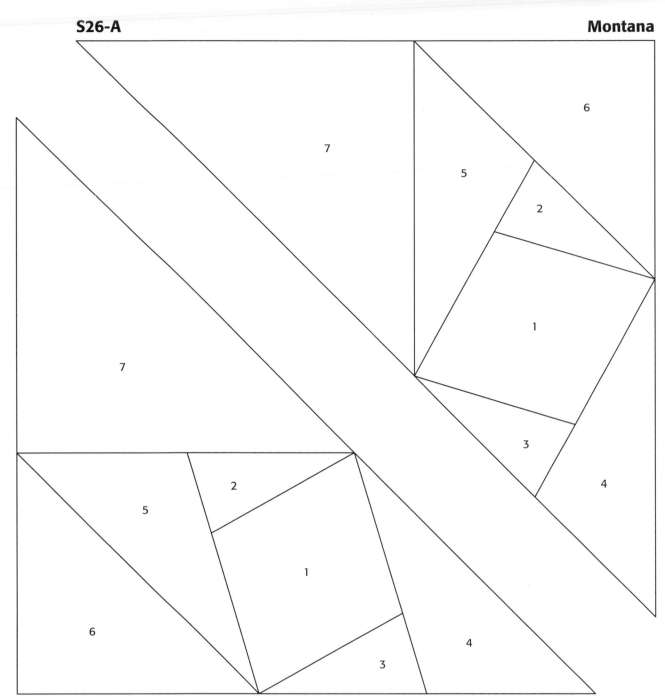

S26-B

Block-Front Drawings

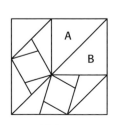

Make 4.

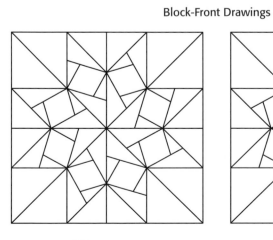

Nebraska Star

48 PIECES

The following cutting list is for one star block.

Fabric	No. of Pieces	Dimensions	Location Numbers	Section
Blue #1	8	2" x 4"	1	A, B
Blue #2	8	2" x 7½"	4	A, B
White	16	2" x 4"	2, 3	A, B
Dark green	2	3¾" x 3¾" ◻	5	A
	2	4¾" x 4¾" ◻	6	A
Medium green	2	3¾" x 3¾" ◻	5	B
	2	4¾" x 4¾" ◻	6	B

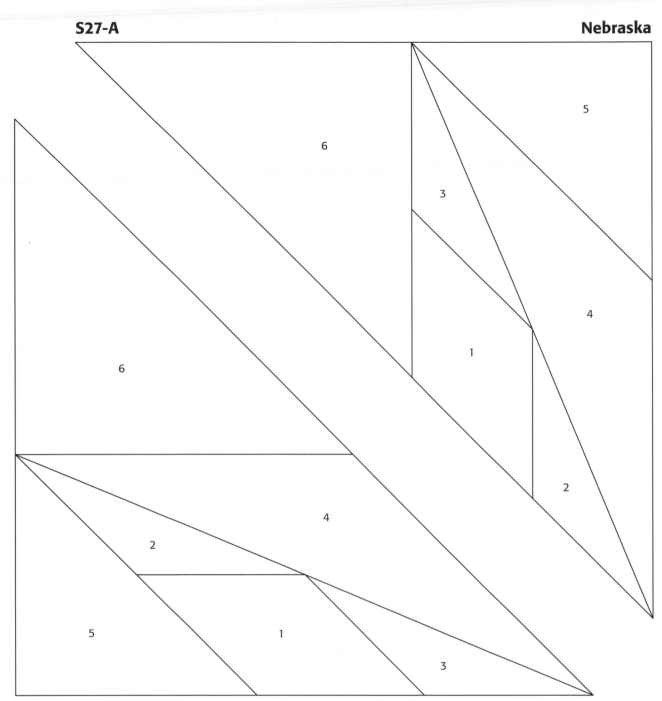

S27-B

Block-Front Drawings

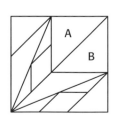

Make 4.

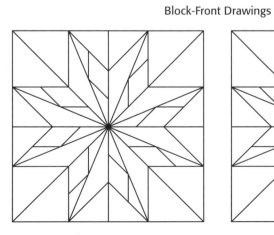

STAR BLOCK 28

Nevada Star

60 PIECES

The following cutting list is for one star block.

Fabric	No. of Pieces	Dimensions	Location Numbers	Section
Light teal	8	2" x 5½"	1	A, B
Black print	16	1½" x 5½"	2, 3	A, B
	2	3¼" x 3¼" ⧅	8*	A, B
Dark teal	8	2½" x 2½"	4	A, B
Pink	8	2" x 4½"	7	A, B
White print	4	3¾" x 3¾" ⧅	5	A, B
	8	2¼" x 4½"	6	A, B

*Add these pieces after sections A and B are joined. See page 18.

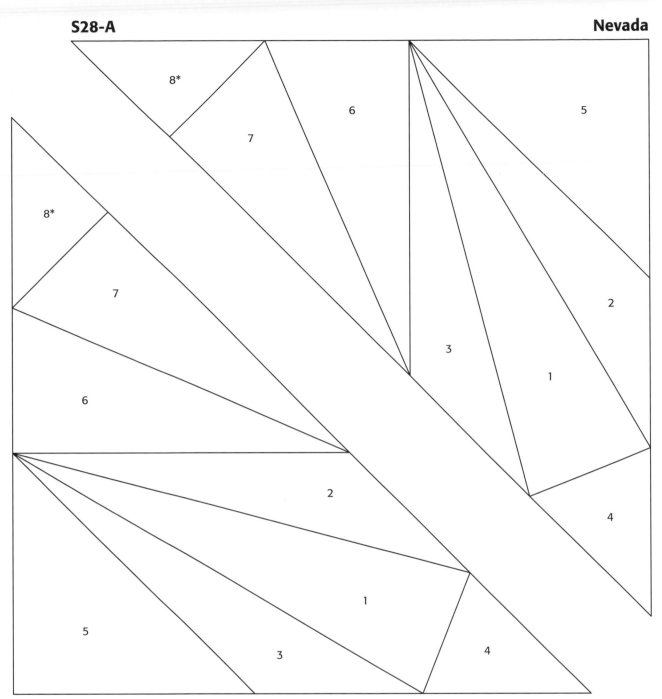

S28-B

8*

6

5

7

8*

3

7

2

1

6

1

2

5

3

4

4

Block-Front Drawings

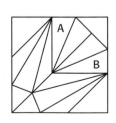

A

B

Make 4.

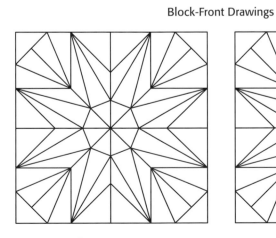

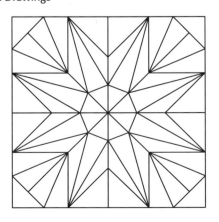

NEW HAMPSHIRE STAR

96 PIECES

The following cutting list is for one star block.

Fabric	No. of Pieces	Dimensions	Location Numbers	Section
Gold	4	1" x 1½"	1	A
Black	8	1¼" x 2"	2, 3	A
	8	1¼" x 3½"	6, 7	A
	24	1¼" x 2½"	10, 11	A
			4, 5, 8, 9	B
	4	2" x 4"	1	B
Dark reds*	4	2" x 3"	4	A
Medium reds*	4	2" x 5"	5	A
Green #1	4	1¼" x 3½"	2	B
Green #2	4	1¼" x 4"	3	B
Green #3	8	1¼" x 4"	8	A
			6	B
Green #4	8	1¼" x 5"	9	A
			7	B
Light green	4	3¾" x 3¾" ◻	12	A
			10	B
	4	4¾" x 4¾" ◻	13	A
			11	B

*To add variety, four different dark red and four different medium red fabrics were used.

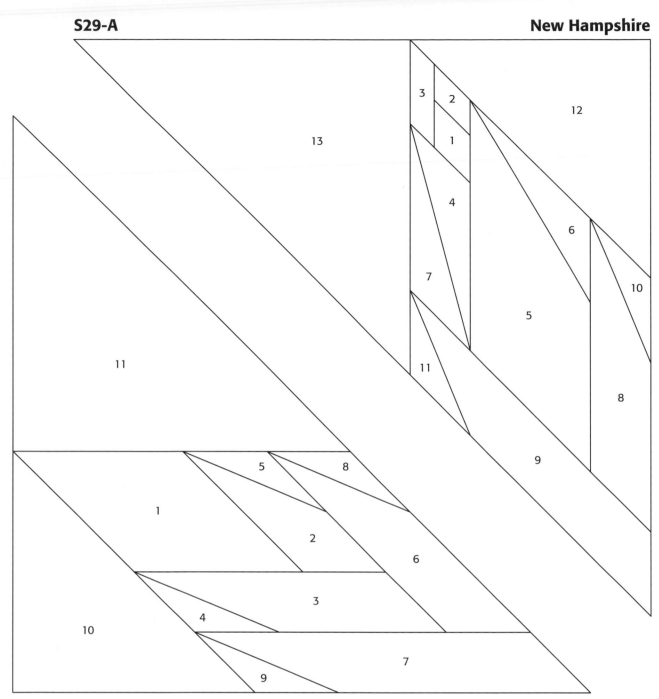

S29-B

Block-Front Drawings

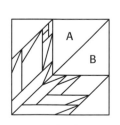

Make 4.

New Jersey Star

72 PIECES

The following cutting list is for one star block.

Fabric	No. of Pieces	Dimensions	Location Numbers	Section
Gold	8	2" x 2"	1	A, B
Light blue	8	2½" x 2½" ◻	2, 3	A, B
	8	2½" x 4"	6	A, B
Medium blue	4	1¼" x 2½"	4	A
Dark blue	4	2" x 3½"	5	A
Medium pink	4	1¼" x 2½"	4	B
Dark pink	4	2" x 3½"	5	B
Dark green	4	2½" x 4½"	7	A
Medium green	4	2½" x 4½"	7	B
Floral	4	3¾" x 3¾" ◻	8	A, B
	4	4¾" x 4¾" ◻	9	A, B

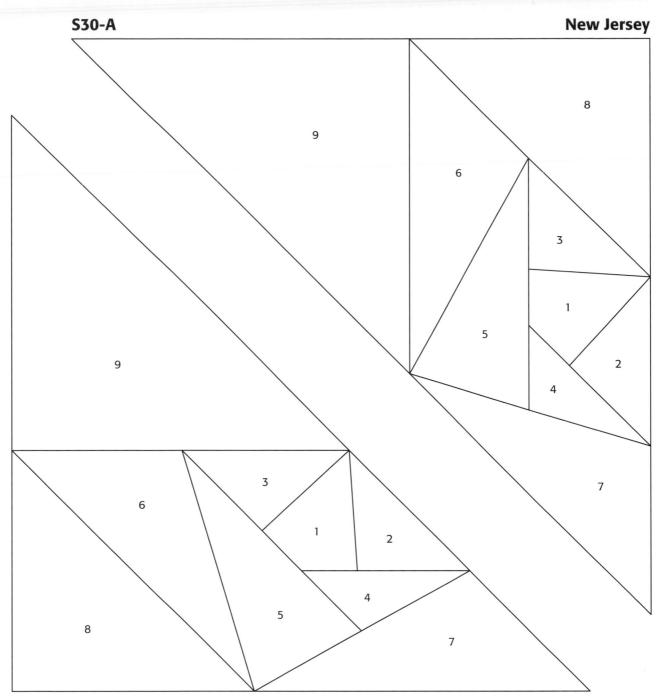

S30-B

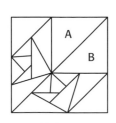

Make 4.

Block-Front Drawings

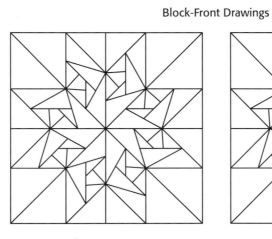

New Mexico Star

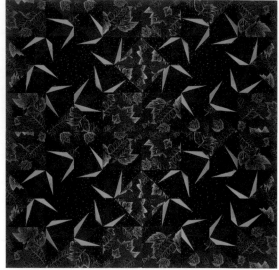

72 PIECES

The following cutting list is for one star block.

Fabric	No. of Pieces	Dimensions	Location Numbers	Section
Red	8	2" x 3½"	1	A, B
Black	16	2" x 3"	2, 3	A, B
	8	3¼" x 3¼" ◱	6, 7	A, B
Gold	16	1" x 3½"	4, 5	A, B
Leaf print	4	3¾" x 3¾" ◱	8	A, B
	4	4¾" x 4¾" ◱	9	A, B

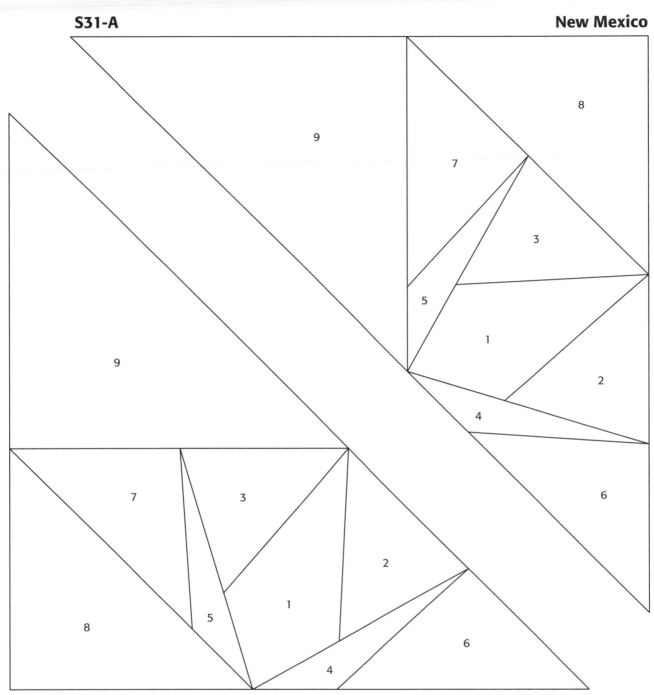

S31-B

Block-Front Drawings

Make 4.

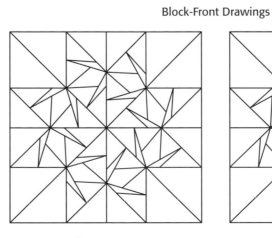

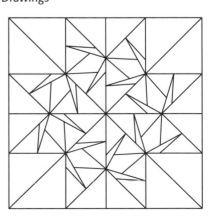

New York Star

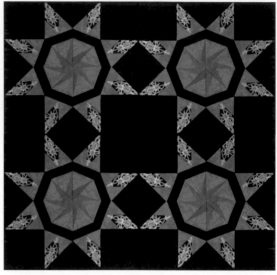

64 PIECES

The following cutting list is for one star block.

Fabric	No. of Pieces	Dimensions	Location Numbers	Section
Large-scale print	8	2½" x 4½"	1†	A, B
Turquoise	16	2" x 3"	2, 3	A, B
	8	2¼" x 3¼	5	A, B
Pink	8	1½" x 4"	6	A, B
Black	8	1½" x 4"	4	A, B
	4	3¾" x 3¾" ◻	7	A, B
	4	4¾" x 4¾" ◻	8	A, B

† The same motif is centered in area #1. See page 9.

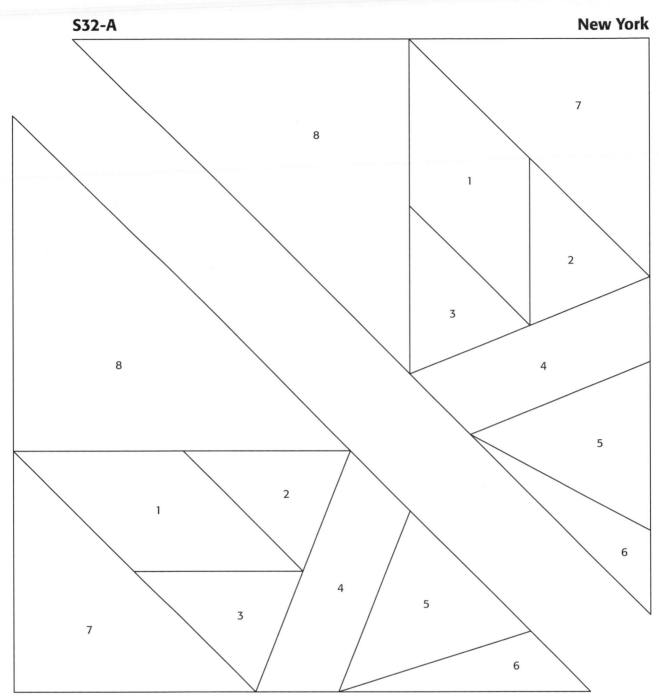

8

7

1

2

3

4

5

8

6

1

2

3

4

5

7

6

S32-B

Block-Front Drawings

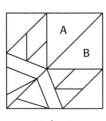

A

B

Make 4.

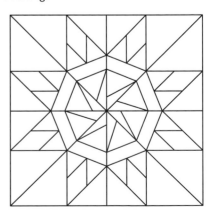

North Carolina Star

72 PIECES

The following cutting list is for one star block.

Fabric	No. of Pieces	Dimensions	Location Numbers	Section
Beige	8	2" x 2½"	1	A, B
	16	1½" x 2"	4, 5	A, B
Light purple	4	1¼" x 4"	3	A
Light green	4	1¼" x 3"	2	A
Medium green	4	1¼" x 4"	3	B
Medium purple	4	1¼" x 3"	2	B
Purple print	8	1½" x 4"	6	A, B
Floral	8	3" x 3"	7	A, B
Dark purple	4	3¾" x 3¾" ◻	8	A, B
	4	4¾" x 4¾" ◻	9	A, B

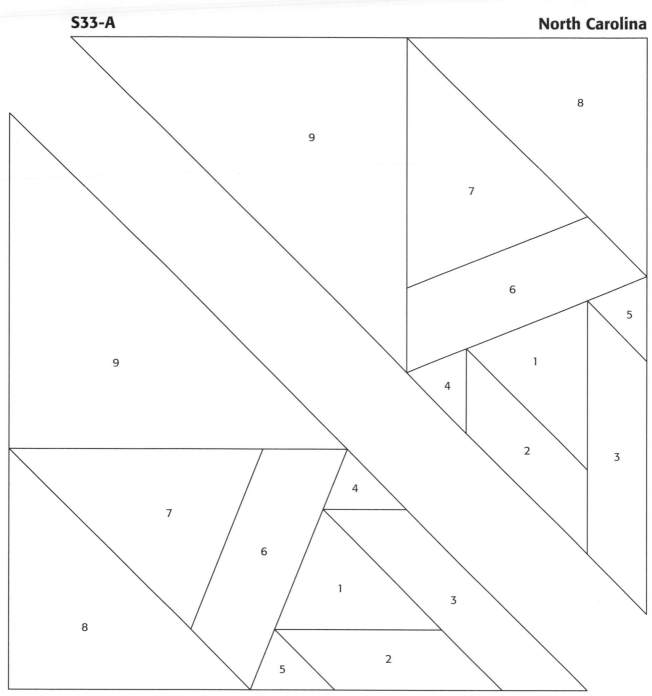

S33-B

Block-Front Drawings

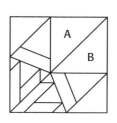

Make 4.

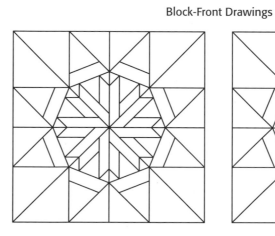

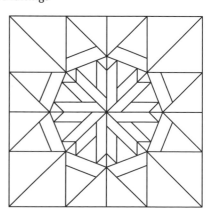

North Dakota Star

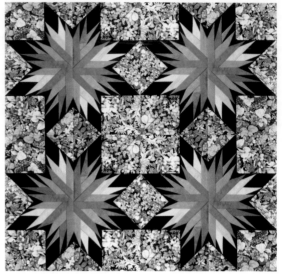

88 PIECES

The following cutting list is for one star block.

Fabric	No. of Pieces	Dimensions	Location Numbers	Section
Black	8	2" x 3¾"	1	A, B
	24	1¼" x 2½"	4, 5	B
			8, 9	A, B
	8	1¼" x 3½"	4, 5	A
Green #1	4	1¼" x 3¼"	2	B
Green #2	4	1¼" x 4"	3	B
Green #3	8	1¼" x 4"	6	A, B
Green #4	8	1¼" x 5"	7	A, B
Pink	4	1¼" x 3¼"	2	A
Lavender	4	1¼" x 4"	3	A
Floral	4	3¾" x 3¾" ◻	10	A, B
	4	4¾" x 4¾" ◻	11	A, B

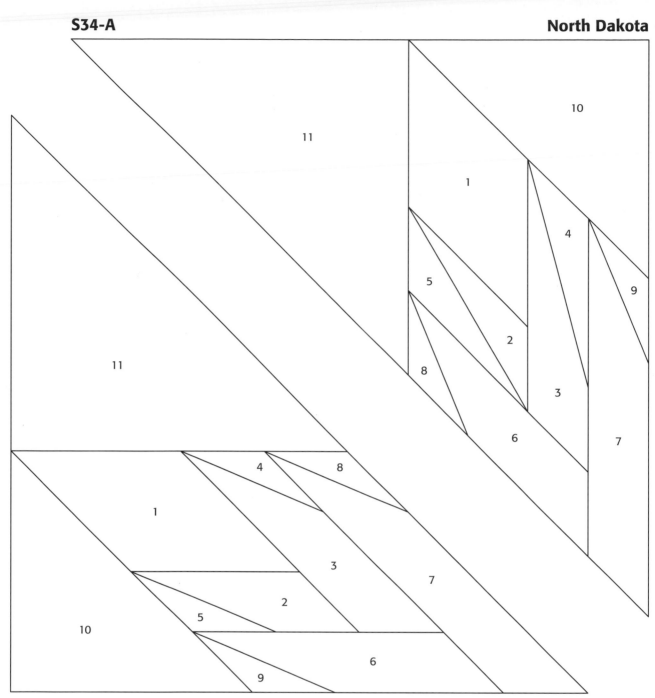

11

11

10

1

4

5

2

9

8

3

6

7

S34-B

1

4

8

3

7

2

5

10

9

6

Block-Front Drawings

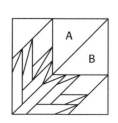

A

B

Make 4.

OHIO STAR

72 PIECES

The following cutting list is for one star block.

Fabric	No. of Pieces	Dimensions	Location Numbers	Section
Red	8	2" x 4"	1	A, B
	8	1¼" x 4"	4	A, B
	8	1¼" x 5"	5	A, B
White	8	1¼" x 3¼"	2	A, B
	8	1¼" x 4"	3	A, B
	16	1¼" x 2¾"	6, 7	A, B
	4	3¾" x 3¾" ◳	8	A, B
	4	4¾" x 4¾" ◳	9	A, B

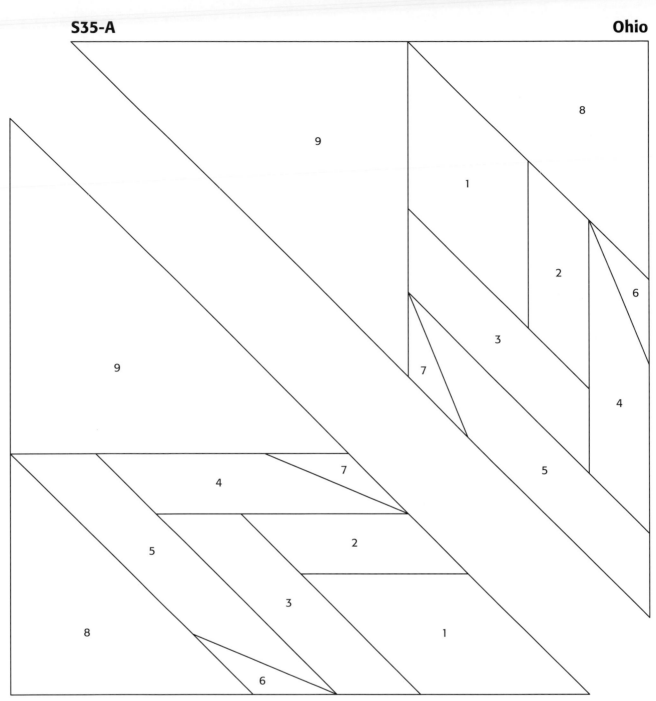

S35-B

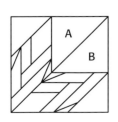

Make 4.

Block-Front Drawings

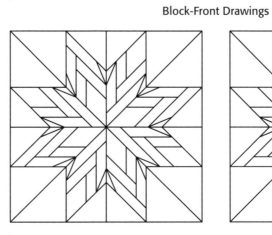

OKLAHOMA STAR

128 PIECES

The following cutting list is for one star block.

Fabric	No. of Pieces	Dimensions	Location Numbers	Section
Dark green	16	1¼" x 5"	13, 14	A, B
Medium-dark green	8	1¼" x 2½"	1	A, B
Medium green	8	1¼" x 2½"	4	A, B
Medium-light green	8	1¼" x 2½"	7	A, B
Light green	8	1¼" x 2½"	10	A, B
White print	32	1¼" x 2¼"	3, 6, 9, 12	A, B
	32	1½" x 1½"	2, 5, 8, 11	A, B
	4	3¾" x 3¾" ◩	15	A, B
	4	4¾" x 4¾" ◪	16	A, B

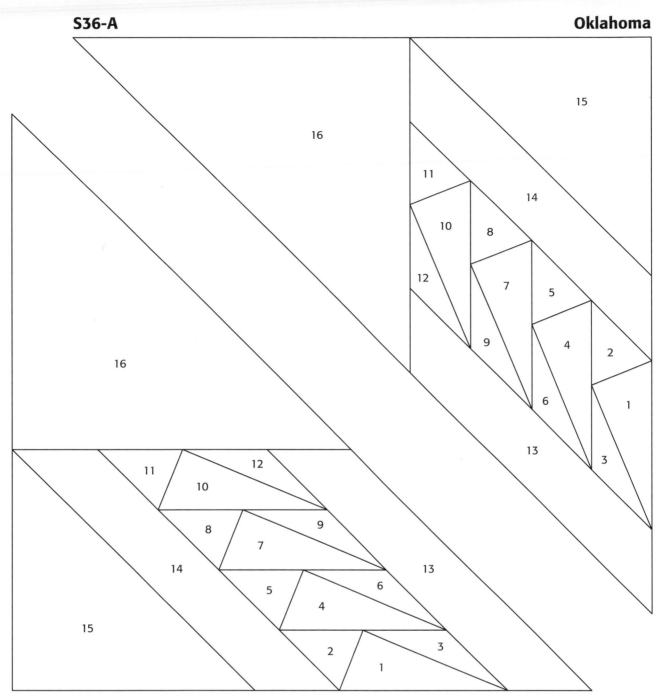

S36-B

Block-Front Drawings

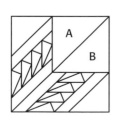

Make 4.

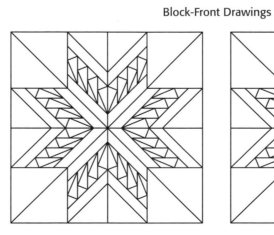

OREGON STAR

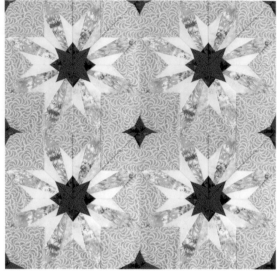

64 PIECES

The following cutting list is for one star block.

Fabric	No. of Pieces	Dimensions	Location Numbers	Section
Floral	8	2" x 6"	1	A, B
White	16	1½" x 4½"	2, 3	A, B
Dark green	4	1½" x 2¼"	8	B
	8	1¼" x 2"	4	A, B
Dark pink	4	1¼" x 2¼"	8	A
	8	1½" x 3¼"	5	A, B
Light pink	4	3¾" x 3¾" ◻	6	A, B
	4	4¾" x 4¾" ◻	7	A, B

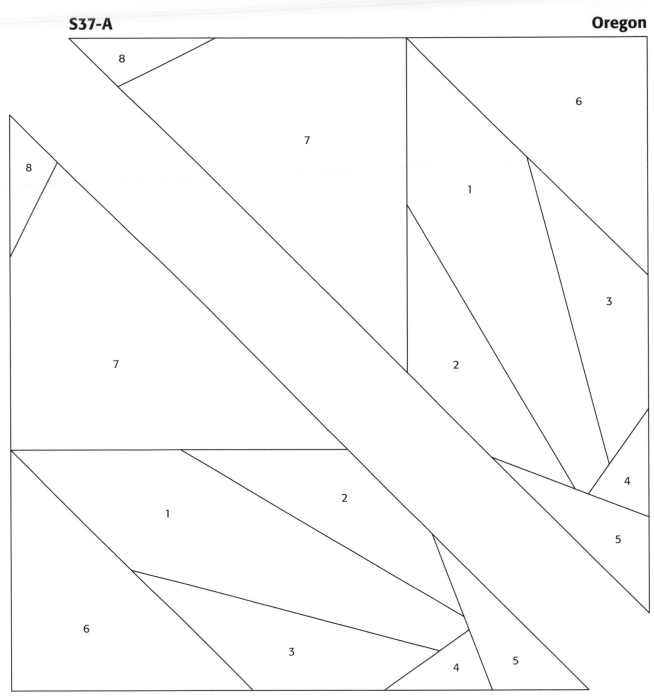

S37-B

Block-Front Drawings

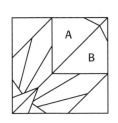

Make 4.

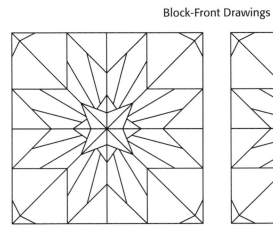

PENNSYLVANIA STAR

64 PIECES

The following cutting list is for one star block.

Fabric	No. of Pieces	Dimensions	Location Numbers	Section
Medium green	8	2" x 4½"	1	A, B
Medium blue	8	2" x 4½"	4	A, B
Yellow	16	1½" x 2½"	2, 5	A, B
White print	16	1¼" x 3½"	3, 6	A, B
	4	3¾" x 3¾" ◿	7	A, B
	4	4¾" x 4¾" ◿	8	A, B

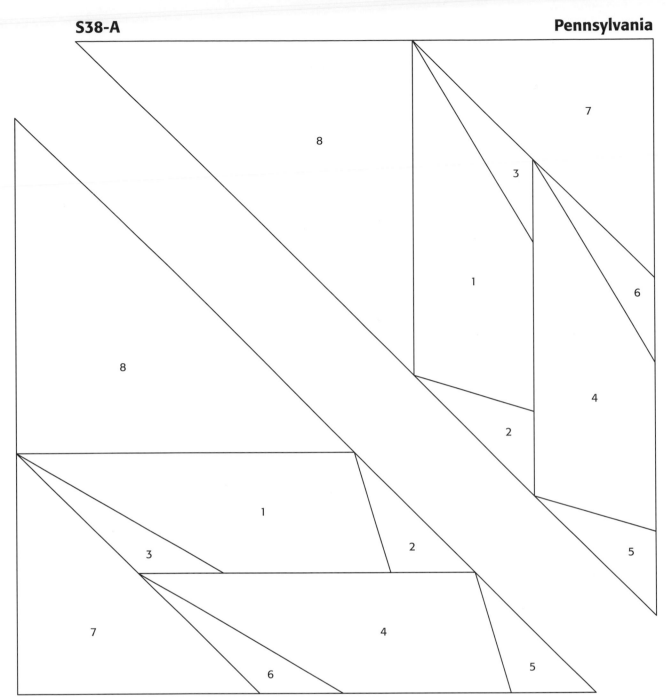

S38-B

Block-Front Drawings

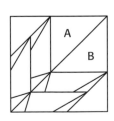

Make 4.

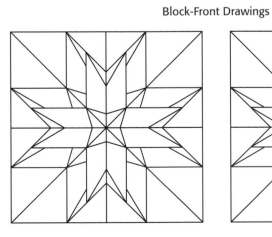

RHODE ISLAND STAR

64 PIECES

The following cutting list is for one star block.

Fabric	No. of Pieces	Dimensions	Location Numbers	Section
Floral	8	2" x 5"	1	A, B
Black	8	2" x 5"	4	A, B
Medium blue	4	2" x 2½"	5	A
Aqua blue	4	2" x 2½"	5	B
Light blue	16	1¼" x 3½"	3, 6	A, B
	8	2" x 2½"	2	A, B
	4	3¾" x 3¾" ◹	7	A, B
	4	4¾" x 4¾" ◹	8	A, B

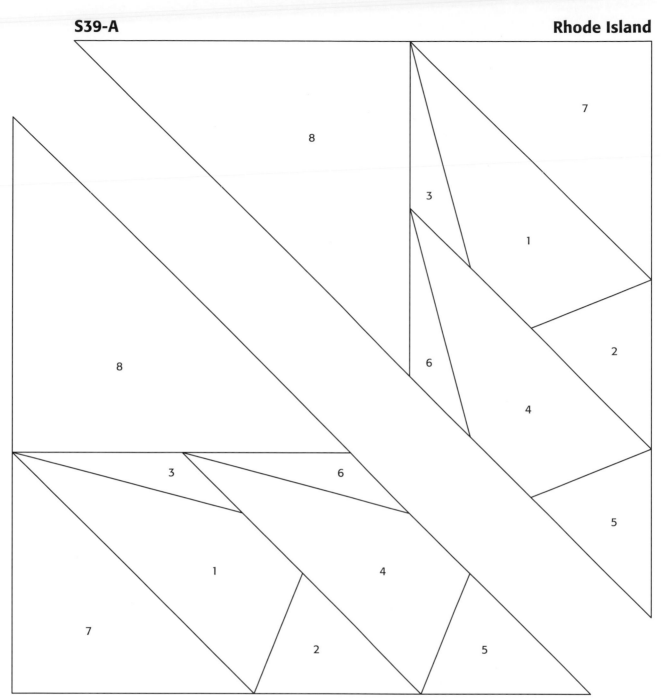

S39-B

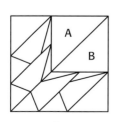

Make 4.

Block-Front Drawings

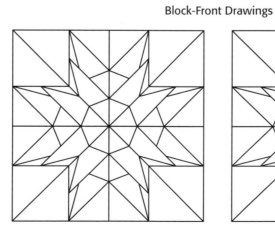

SOUTH CAROLINA STAR

120 PIECES

The following cutting list is for one star block.

Fabric	No. of Pieces	Dimensions	Location Numbers	Section
Dark pink	8	1¼" x 5"	12	A, B
	8	1¼" x 2¼"	6	A, B
Medium pink	8	1¼" x 5"	10	A, B
	8	1¼" x 2¼"	4	A, B
Medium-light pink	8	1¼" x 5"	8	A, B
	8	1¼" x 2¼"	2	A, B
Navy blue	56	1¼" x 2¼"	1, 3, 5, 7,	A, B
			9, 11,13	A, B
	4	3¾" x 3¾" ◻	14	A, B
	4	4¾" x 4¾" ◻	15	A, B

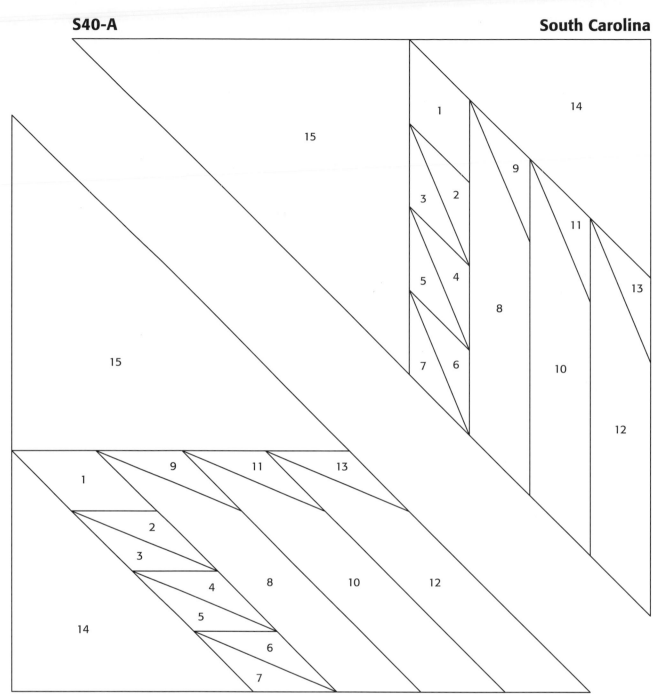

15

1

14

15

9

3 2

11

5 4

13

8

7 6

10

12

9

11

13

1

2

3

4 8 10 12

5

14

6

7

S40-B

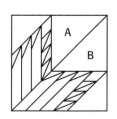

A

B

Make 4.

Block-Front Drawings

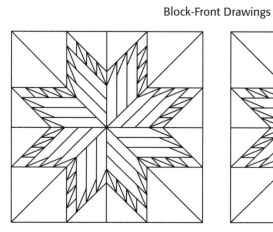

South Dakota Star

100 PIECES

The following cutting list is for one star block.

Fabric	No. of Pieces	Dimensions	Location Numbers	Section
Red	8	2" x 4"	1	A, B
	32	1¼" x 3"	4, 5, 8, 9	A, B
	2	2½" x 2½" ◻	13*	A, B
Dark green #1	8	1¼" x 4¼"	3	A, B
	8	1½" x 4"	12	A, B
Dark green #2	8	1¼" x 5¼"	7	A, B
Medium green #1	8	1¼" x 3¼"	2	A, B
Medium green #2	8	1¼" x 4½"	6	A, B
White print	4	3¾" x 3¾" ◻	10	A, B
	8	3" x 4½"	11	A, B

*Add these pieces after sections A and B are joined. See page 18.

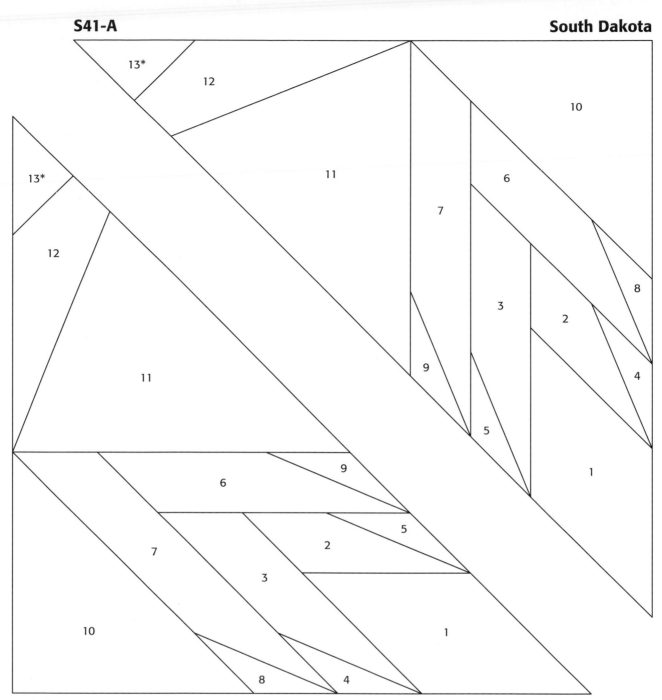

S41-B

Block-Front Drawings

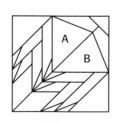

Make 4.

Tennessee Star

64 PIECES

The following cutting list is for one star block.

Fabric	No. of Pieces	Dimensions	Location Numbers	Section
Green	8	1½" x 2½"	2	A, B
	4	1½" x 3½"	7	A
Dark wine	8	2½" x 4"	3	A, B
Wine	8	1¼" x 3½"	5	A, B
	4	1½" x 3½"	7	B
Brown	8	1¼" x 2½"	4	A, B
White print	8	4" x 4"	1†	A, B
	4	3¾" x 3¾" ◻	8	A, B
	4	4¾" x 4¾" ◻	6	A, B

† The same motif is centered in area #1. See page 9.

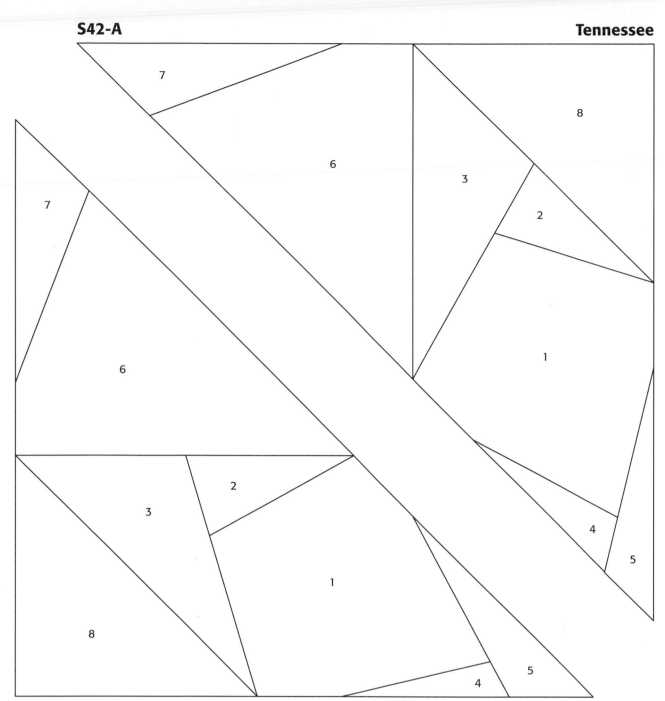

S42-B

Block-Front Drawings

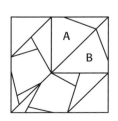

Make 4.

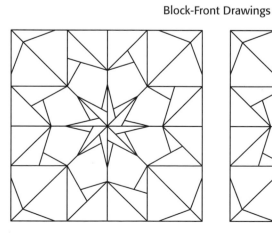
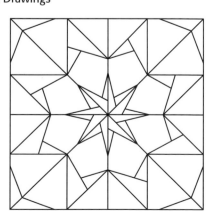

Texas Star

68 PIECES

The following cutting list is for one star block.

Fabric	No. of Pieces	Dimensions	Location Numbers	Section
Red	8	1¼" x 4"	2	A, B
Rust floral	4	1½" x 6"	8*	A, B
	2	3" x 3" ◻	10*	A, B
Peach	8	1¼" x 5"	3	A, B
	4	1¼" x 4"	9*	A, B
Dark green	8	2½" x 5¼"	1	A, B
	16	1¼" x 2½"	4, 5	A, B
	8	3¾" x 3¾" ◻	6, 7	A, B

*Add these pieces after sections A and B are joined. See page 18.

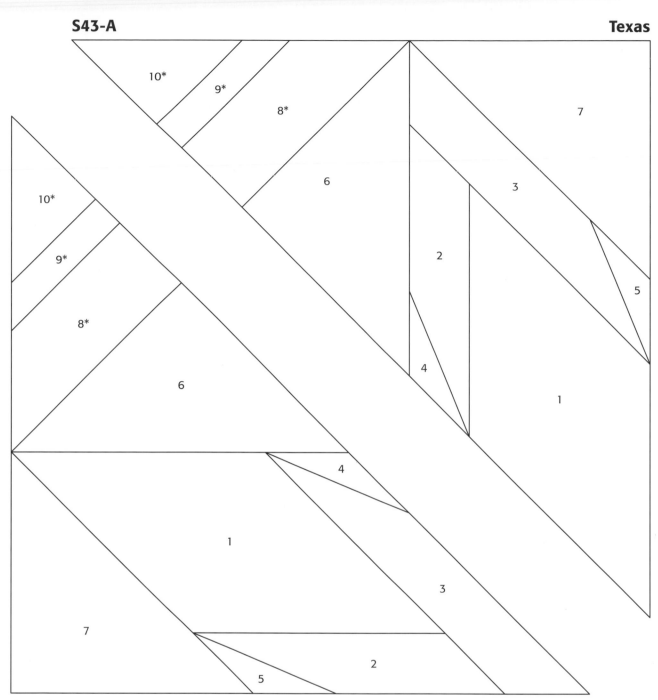

10*

9*

8*

7

6

3

2

5

10*

9*

4

8*

1

6

4

1

3

7

2

5

S43-B

Block-Front Drawings

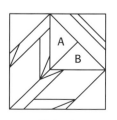

A

B

Make 4.

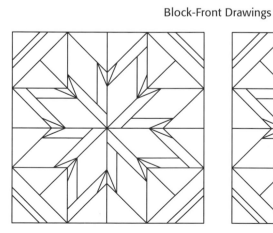

UTAH STAR

64 PIECES

The following cutting list is for one star block.

Fabric	No. of Pieces	Dimensions	Location Numbers	Section
Dark blue	4	1½" x 3¼"	2	B
Medium blue	4	2" x 4"	1	A
Light blue	4	1½" x 4¼"	4	B
	4	1½" x 5"	5	B
	4	2" x 2"	4	A
	4	3½" x 4½"	5	A
Green	4	1½" x 4¼"	3	B
	4	2¼" x 2¼" ◻	7	A, B
Beige print	4	2" x 4"	1	B
	8	1½" x 2½"	2, 3	A
	4	3¾" x 3¾" ◻	6	A, B
	4	4¾" x 4¾" ◻	8	A, B

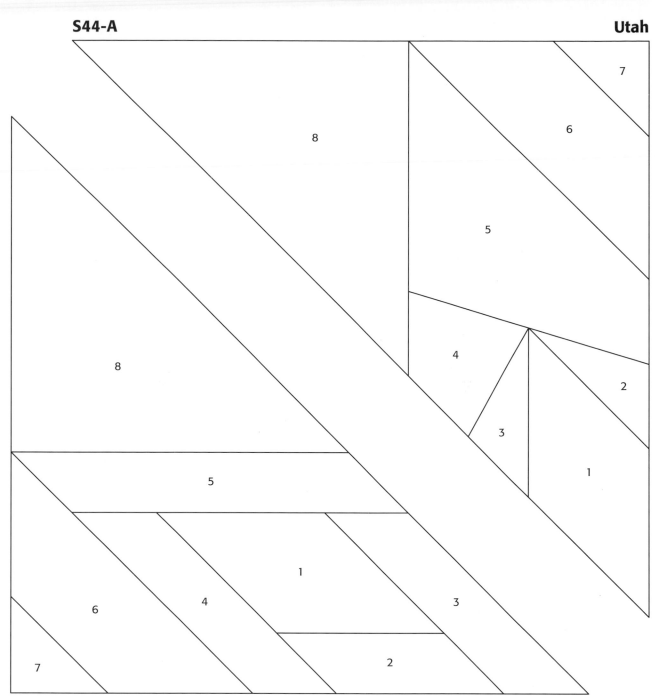

S44-A

7

6

8

5

4

2

3

1

8

5

1

4

3

6

2

7

S44-B

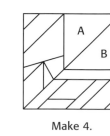

A

B

Make 4.

Block-Front Drawings

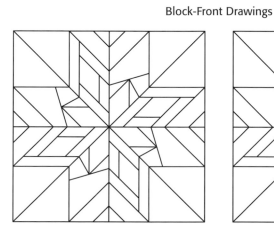

VERMONT STAR

64 PIECES

The following cutting list is for one star block.

Fabric	No. of Pieces	Dimensions	Location Numbers	Section
White	8	2" x 4"	1	A, B
Medium blue	4	2" x 4"	2	B
	4	1½" x 4"	3	A
Dark blue	4	1½" x 4"	3	B
	4	2" x 4"	2	A
Dark green	4	2" x 6"	4	B
Medium green	4	2" x 6"	4	A
	8	1¼" x 4¾"	5	A, B
	4	1¼" x 6½"	8*	A, B
Light green	4	3¼" x 3¼" ◻	6	A, B
	4	3¾" x 3¾" ◻	7	A, B
	2	4" x 4" ◻	9*	A, B

*Add these pieces after sections A and B are joined. See page 18.

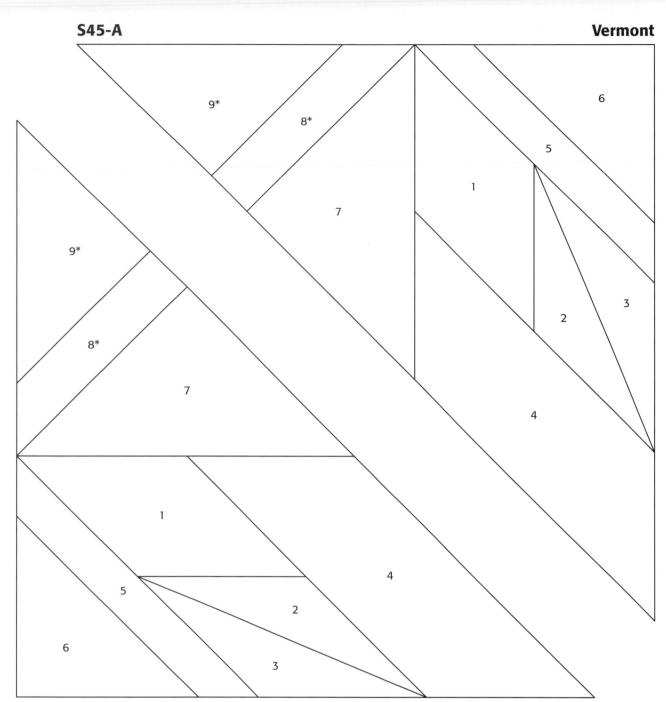

S45-B

Block-Front Drawings

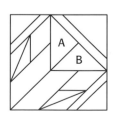

Make 4.

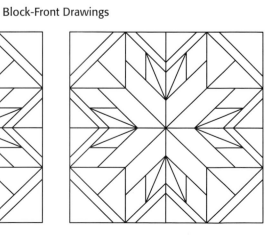

VIRGINIA STAR

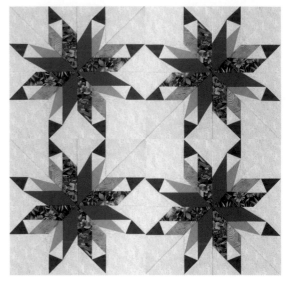

56 PIECES

The following cutting list is for one star block.

Fabric	No. of Pieces	Dimensions	Location Numbers	Section
Medium green	4	2" x 4"	1	B
Floral	4	2" x 6"	3	B
Light pink	4	2" x 3¾"	1	A
Dark pink	4	2" x 6"	3	A
Dark green	8	2½" x 2½"	4	A, B
Beige print	8	2" x 2½"	2	A, B
	8	1¼" x 4"	5, 6	A
	4	3¾" x 3¾" ◱	7	A
			5	B
	4	4¾" x 4¾" ◱	8	A
			6	B

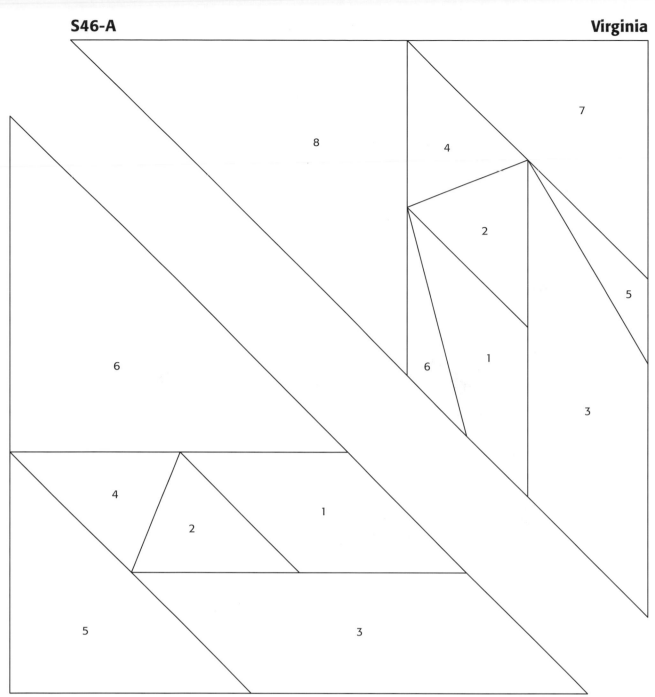

S46-B

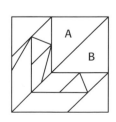

Make 4.

Block-Front Drawings

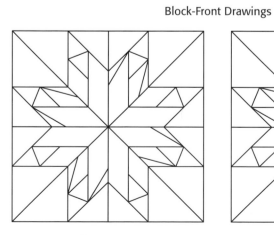

WASHINGTON STAR

64 PIECES

The following cutting list is for one star block.

Fabric	No. of Pieces	Dimensions	Location Numbers	Section
Gold	8	2" x 4"	2	A, B
Rust	8	2" x 4½"	3	A, B
Dark green	8	2" x 4"	1	A, B
	16	1½" x 4"	4, 5	A, B
	8	2½" x 2½"	6	A, B
White print	4	3¾" x 3¾" ◻	7	A, B
	4	4¾" x 4¾" ◻	8	A, B

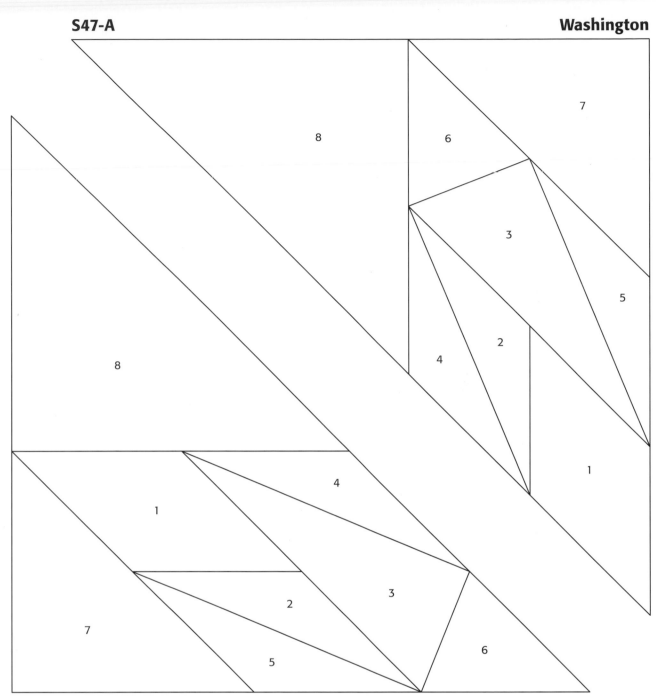

S47-B

Block-Front Drawings

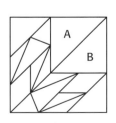

Make 4.

West Virginia Star

108 PIECES

The following cutting list is for one star block.

Fabric	No. of Pieces	Dimensions	Location Numbers	Section
Pink	8	2¼" x 3"	1	A, B
Purple	8	1¼" x 3"	11	A, B
Light teal	16	1½" x 3"	4, 5	A, B
Medium teal	16	1½" x 3"	8, 9	A, B
Black	32	1½" x 2"	2, 3, 6, 7	A, B
	2	3" x 3" ◹	14*	A, B
	4	2½" x 2½" ◹	10	A, B
Floral	4	3¾" x 3¾" ◹	12	A, B
	4	4¾" x 4¾" ◹	13	A, B

*Add these pieces after sections A and B are joined. See page 18.

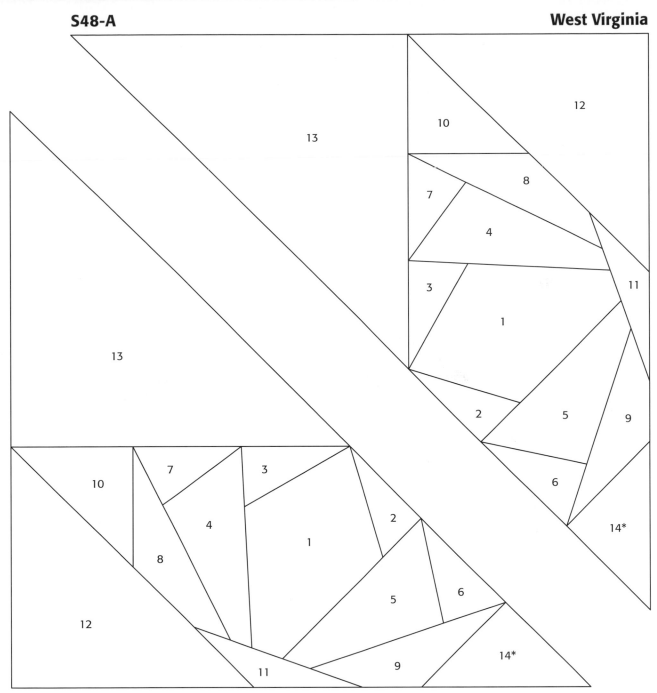

S48-B

Block-Front Drawings

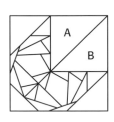

Make 4.

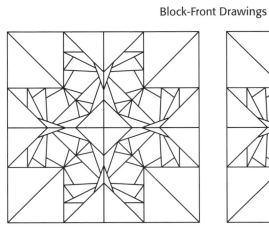

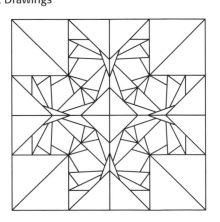

Wisconsin Star

56 PIECES

The following cutting list is for one star block.

Fabric	No. of Pieces	Dimensions	Location Numbers	Section
Navy	8	2½" x 3½"	1	A, B
Blue floral	8	3" x 3"	2	A, B
Gold	8	1½" x 2½"	3	A, B
Medium blue	8	1½" x 3½"	4	A, B
Dark blue	8	2½" x 2½"	5	A, B
Light blue	4	3¾" x 3¾" ◻	6	A, B
	4	4¾" x 4¾" ◻	7	A, B

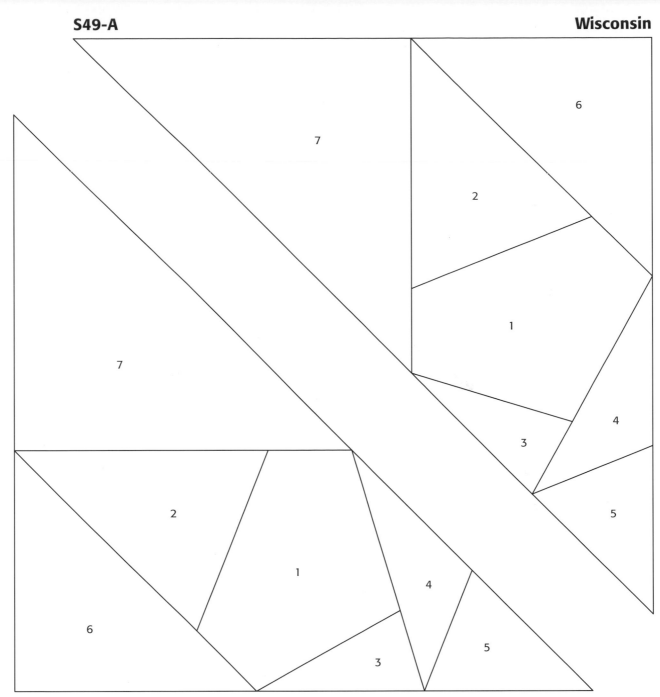

S49-B

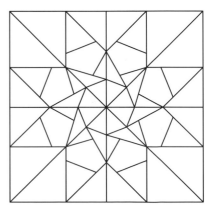

Block-Front Drawings

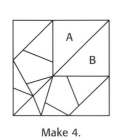

Make 4.

WYOMING STAR

72 PIECES

The following cutting list is for one star block.

Fabric	No. of Pieces	Dimensions	Location Numbers	Section
Medium blue	4	1½" x 3"	10	B
	8	1¼" x 3"	2, 3	B
	8	2½" x 2½"	4	A
			7	B
Dark blue	8	2½" x 2½"	5	A
			4	B
	4	1½" x 3"	8	A
	16	1¼" x 3"	2, 3	A
			5, 6	B
White print	4	3¾" x 3¾"	1	B
	4	3½" x 4"	1	A
	4	3¾" x 3¾" 	6	A
			8	B
	4	4¾" x 4¾" 	7	A
			9	B

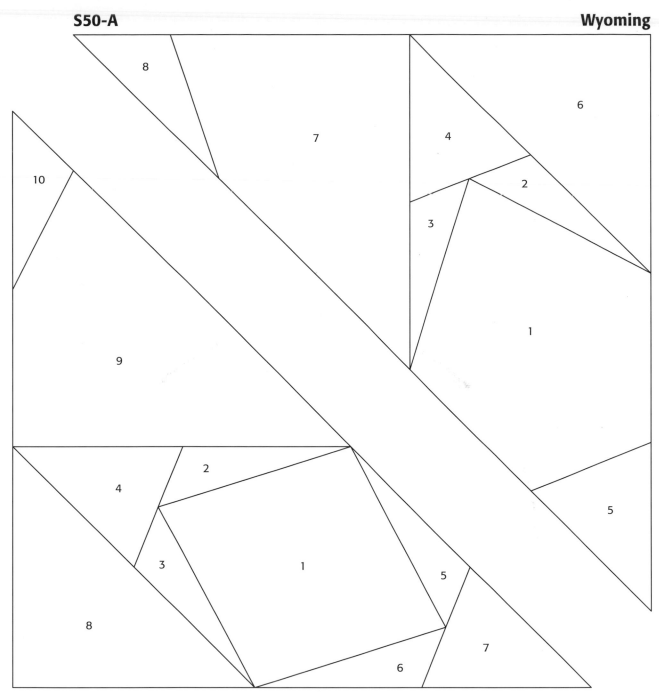

S50-B

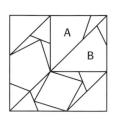

Make 4.

Block-Front Drawings

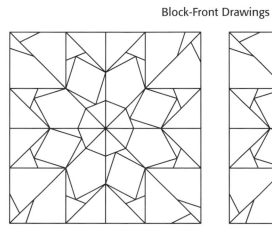

RESOURCES

Papers for Foundation Piecing and the 6" Add-a-Quarter ruler are available from:

Martingale & Company
PO Box 118
Bothell, WA 98041-0118
USA
(1-800-426-3126)

The 50 *Fabulous Paper-Pieced Stars* Companion Software CD-ROM is available by sending a check, payable to Quilt-Pro Systems, for $14.95 plus $3.00 shipping and handling to:

50 Fabulous Stars Software
PO Box 560692
The Colony, TX 75056

Or order via a credit card on the Web at:
www.CarolDoak.com/order

System Requirements: Windows 95/98/NT4, 8 MB RAM, 25 MB available disk space, mouse or other pointing device. High-color or true-color video recommended.

ABOUT THE AUTHOR

*A*S A BESTSELLING author, celebrated teacher, lecturer, and award-winning quiltmaker, Carol Doak has greatly influenced the art and craft of quiltmaking for more than a decade, both in the U.S. and internationally. Her accomplishments include a sizable collection of popular books: *Easy Machine Paper Piecing, Easy Paper-Pieced Keepsake Quilts, Easy Mix & Match Machine Paper Piecing, Show Me How to Paper Piece, Easy Reversible Vests, Easy Paper-Pieced Miniatures, Your First Quilt Book (or it should be!)* and *Easy Stash Quilts.* Sales are quickly approaching half a million books in print! It is no secret that Carol has helped to raise the popularity of paper piecing, her trademark technique, to heights never before seen in the world of quiltmaking.

An impressive range of her beautiful blue-ribbon quilts has been featured in several books, such as *Great American Quilts 1990* and *The Quilt Encyclopedia,* and on the covers of *Quilter's Newsletter Magazine, Quilt World, Quilting Today, Ladies' Circle Patchwork* and *McCall's Quilting.*

If you have ever taken a class from Carol, you know that her enthusiasm for quiltmaking is infectious. Carol has a gift of sharing her inspiring ideas with her students in a positive and unique way.

Carol lives in Windham, New Hampshire, where she claims the cold winters give her plenty of reason to stockpile a fabric stash for insulation purposes!